COLOSSIANS & PHILEMON

A PARTICIPATORY STUDY GUIDE

ALLAN R. BEVERE

Energion Publications
Gonzalez, FL
2016

ISBN10: 1-63199-223-6
ISBN13: 978-1-63199-223-0
Library of Congress Control Number: 2016935332

Energion Publications
P. O. Box 841
Gonzalez, FL 32560

energion.com
pubs@energion.com

PRAISE FOR COLOSSIANS & PHILEMON: A PARTICIPATORY STUDY GUIDE

As a pastor I am always on the lookout for solid material for small groups and other teaching opportunities. Allan R. Bevere's *Colossians & Philemon: A Participatory Study Guide* is one that I would certainly recommend for my local church. I have seen a fair share of Bible studies focus more on the questions while being devoid of any understanding of context of the original author or original audience. Bevere's study brings these elements to the forefront which provides the group with a more focused and clearer understanding of the meaning of the epistle in its proper setting. I also appreciated the simple but very practical application "exercises" associated with each study. As a pastor I am always trying to encourage the congregation to live out what they are learning. This addition provides an opportunity to apply what is taught along with group accountability. This study will prove to be a valuable ministry tool.

– Rev. Christopher J. Freet
DMin. student (Biblical Seminary)
Pastor at Millersville Brethren in Christ Church
Author of *A New Look at Hospitality as a Key to Missions*

Dr. Allan Bevere has masterfully struck a perfect balance between history, theology, and modern scholarship that undergirds Paul's letters to the church in Colossae and his friend, Philemon. Allan outlines for us the clear connection between the two letters while highlighting the practical theological issues both were facing. Allan's attention to detail helps the reader draw closer to the personal issues of the early church while providing a pastoral path for individual spiritual growth and Christian maturity. This is a perfect participatory study for those seeking to deepen their faith in Christ.

– Dr. Robert C. McKibben
Retired United Methodist Pastor
Author of *Holy Smoke! Unholy Fire!* and *Mark: A Participatory Study Guide* (forthcoming)
Emmaus Spiritual Director

I've read many commentaries on Colossians and Philemon but this one is probably one of the best. The most obvious asset is its conciseness. Allan gets to his point quickly and without unnecessary jargon. The book is also unique in the way it presents Paul as a scholar-missionary who was interested in far more than head knowledge. His emphasis was always on what Allan calls "incarnational ecclesiology." For Paul, "The gospel is credible only as it is demonstrated by individual saints and the church collectively in the good works that bear witness to God's kingdom." I suspect readers will also enjoy the discussion questions found at the end of each chapter. I could add much more about this book but I urge you to just read it. My thanks to Allan and Energion for making this fine commentary available.

– Dr. David Alan Black
Professor of Greek and New Testament
Dr. M.O. Owens, Jr. Chair of New Testament Studies
Southeastern Baptist Theological Seminary
Author of *Paul, Apostle of Weakness*

TABLE OF CONTENTS

The Book of Colossians feels like an old friend. My formal research on the letter began in 1991 when I started my Ph.D. at the University of Durham in the United Kingdom. My advisor, Jimmy Dunn was beginning to write his own commentary on Colossians and was pleased to have a student of his working on the subject. I was very open to researching Colossians—it was one of my favorite of the Pauline epistles and I wanted to work on the question of the relationship between Christology and ethics. So, I was off and running for the next seven years.

What I did not realize at the time was that for the next twenty-five years I would be devoted to writing and publishing on Colossians. Once my dissertation was published, the invitations to write on the subject started coming regularly. Some I had to turn down simply because I did not have the time, but other invitations were accepted. I wrote chapters and essays here and there, and gave an interview on the connection between Colossians and the modern notion of empire, but in all that time, I had never written a commentary on the book I spent a quarter of a century with in my studies. So, it now seems appropriate to do so after all this time. I hope that you the reader find the finished product worth your time.

As always, there are many people to thank when writing a book. Henry and Jody Neufeld of Energion Publications are great people to work with in the ministry of writing and publishing. And they also have demonstrated the virtue of patience in waiting for this book which was submitted long overdue.

My wife Carol continues to be a great encouragement to me and has at times sent me to my study to write when I would prefer to chill out in front of the TV. She believes in what I do and supports me in my endeavors. I cannot imagine my life without her.

And finally, I am very grateful for the influence and friendship of my *doktorvater*, James D. G. Dunn who helped me enter into the wonderful world of Pauline studies, and particularly of Colossians some twenty-five years ago. I dedicate this commentary to him.

--Allan R. Bevere, September 2015

For Jimmy

USING THIS BOOK

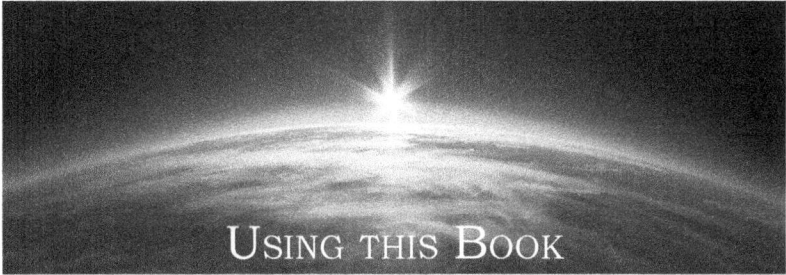

This study guide consists of three sections:

1. Introductory information
2. Lessons
3. Appendices

It is recommended that you first read the *Appendix A: Participatory Bible Study*, to learn the approach to Bible study used in this series. This guide is built around that approach. You may have other ideas, or even a completely different method, and that is fine, but it will still help if you understand the starting point.

You should also have some kind of guideline for how you will approach your study. That guide is going to suggest a process of study, which I'll repeat briefly here:

1. Preparation, including materials, prayer, and opening your mind
2. Overview
3. Background
4. The inner cycle (or central loop): Meditate, Question, Research, Compare
5. Sharing

This is a study process and says very little as such about what you do in each step in the process. It is built on the principles of *lectio divina*, or "holy reading." Let's summarize those principles first and then look at the steps and see how they will help you apply these same principles.

Holy Reading: A Model for Bible Study

Lectio divina, which means holy reading, is an ancient practice of studying scripture. There are many ways to practice *lectio divina*. It has been done in many ways since Origen described it around 220 AD. The great monastic traditions of the church further developed it into distinct phases and practices. The basic principle is that reading and studying the Bible should be remarkably different than reading the morning paper or studying Shakespeare. The Bible is a sacred text; it is a *Living Word*. It should not be studied like it is dead pages from history.

When the two men were walking down the Road to Emmaus, they met the risen Christ, but did not recognize him (Luke 24). As they were walking down the road, Jesus interpreted to them all the scriptures. Only later in the breaking of the bread did they realize that Christ was with them the whole time.

Lectio Divina is a practice that, through the power of the Holy Spirit, invites the risen Christ to interpret scripture to us anew. It is a prayerful reading of scripture that expects God to speak once again through his Holy Word. Prayer should influence the way you study the Bible, and studying the Bible should influence the way you pray. In *lectio divina*, it is impossible to tell when you are studying and when you are praying. There is no difference.

This practice is usually applied on small passages of scripture for an extended period of time. However, in this study *lectio divina* is used as a strategy to study an entire book of the Bible. This is somewhat challenging because the scripture text is so large, but the prayerful approach is still crucial to Christian study of the scripture. In these lessons, the ancient practice of *lectio* is blended with modern study methods that take into account the historical, cultural, and literary contexts.

The historical methods are important to us because they help connect us to people of a different time and place who experienced the same God that we do, learned from the same texts, and were led by the same Spirit. We do not study history because we think history is the meaning; we study history to help us meet those who wrote the texts and those who have studied the passages before us.

The lessons in this guide are designed around the four movements of *lectio divina* established by Guigo II, a 12th century Carthusian monk, in a book called *The Monk's Ladder*. He organized the practice around four rungs that help us draw closer to God through reading the Bible.

Reading (lectio): The first rung of the ladder is reading. Believe it or not this is the step most often skipped or diminished. It is important to do the Bible reading for each lesson in order to get the most out of it. Ideally it should be read several times so that you can become familiar with the language and themes of the text. This book is a guide to help you study the Bible. It is a supplement to the Biblical text; the text itself should have primary focus in your study. The steps of the participatory study method emphasize different ways of reading to help the text become part of you as you study.

Meditating (meditatio): The next thing to do is to prayerfully meditate on the text. Dig deep into it. Study the words. Break it down into pieces. In this study this is where the most of the background information is located. Look up words to find their meaning. Notice if there are any words or actions that the Holy Spirit may be leading you to examine further.

Praying (oratio): Third, we learn to pray the text. Use what you have learned from the scripture to formulate a prayer. It may be helpful to write it down. At the end of each lesson is a prayerful exercise that expounds on one of the themes from the text. Feel free to add your own prayers. This is where the text really becomes alive to us.

In the method used for this study guide, prayer is not seen as simply one part of the study; prayer permeates your study. You start with prayer and listening so that you will hear what God has to say through the text. Then you end by turning what you have heard from God back into prayer. The prayer never ceases!

Contemplating (contemplatio): The last step is the most difficult and rewarding. You have **read** the text, **studied** the text, **prayed** the text. Now it is time to **be** the text. Let it seep into your being. Be still and listen. Make sure you leave some time after the prayer for silence and reflection.

It is said that Dan Rather once interviewed Mother Theresa about her prayer life. Rather asked her, "What do you say to God when you pray?"

Her answer was simple; "I don't say anything; I just listen."

After that he asked, "Well, what does Jesus say to you?"

And Mother Theresa answered, "Oh, He doesn't say anything, either. He just listens."

Listening is what is important. You may not always feel anything, but God is there. Another facet of contemplation is to learn to *do* the text. We cannot be just hearers of the word, we must also be doers of the word. Let the scripture change the way you live your life.

APPLYING THE PRINCIPLES IN PARTICIPATORY STUDY

Preparation

As you begin the study, preparation will involve getting the materials you want to use, then prayer to begin each session of study. Part of this introductory time will be making decisions about the time and resources you can devote to this study. This is also your time of prayer. Before you begin to read, you need to pray. Then you need to listen. You come to the text because God calls you to it.

Overview

Getting the overview is accomplished by reading Colossians through at least once, but preferably three times, and in exceptional cases up to 12 times. Don't feel bad about how many times you read. Choose a number that seems reasonable to you. If you start reading the third time, and it feels like a burden, move on. This is part of *lectio* but only part. You will learn to read in other ways in different phases of your study. Once you have read the Colossian letter through your chosen number of times, read one or two of the following

1. The entry on Colossians in a Bible handbook

2. The entry on Colossians in a Bible dictionary

3. The introductory note on Colossians in your study Bible, if you're using one.

4. The introductory section of a good commentary on Colossians (see Appendix B for resource details)

Here is where we introduce historical elements into your study. Don't imagine that God cannot talk to you through this text because you are so far separated from the people who wrote it. They were people like you who had hopes, dreams, gifts, and failings. Study the background to help you connect to them. Christianity is a community that extends not only in space right now but in time.

THE CENTRAL LOOP

For this overview, your central loop, as I call it, is your whole study of the book. Keep in mind that no element of your study is something you do just once and then forget about it. Prayer is continuous. There are multiple ways of reading, questioning, studying, and sharing.

This is most closely related to *meditatio*, but the implementation of *meditatio* extends into the next section where you question the text in a directed way. Don't concentrate on the boundaries between one activity and the next. They are all related!

With each unit there will be an opportunity to try to think of new questions one might ask for further study. Generating new questions helps keep us from getting stale. Not only do I not have all the answers; I don't even have all the questions! Think of a question primarily as a way to prepare your mind to hear the text.

When we listen or read, we often hear what we expect to hear. If I'm listening to the radio for weather, I may miss a major discussion of politics. You can miss what God is saying to you through a Bible writer because you are looking for something else. Questioning is thus an important part of *meditatio*, but it also relates closely to *oratio*—take your questions to God in prayer.

Finally, find something to share. Remember that sharing can be in the form of a question. For example, one might ask others how they understand a particular word, such as "incarnation," "poverty," or "atonement." Take notes on their answers, and bring that information back to your study. Then ask yourself what your neighbors will hear when you make particular statements, such as "I must be bold for Jesus!" or "Jesus is the only way to receive atonement." Do those statements mean something to them? Do they mean the same thing to them as they do to you?

This is part of *contemplatio*, as you try to be and do the text. We often think of sharing primarily as telling someone things that we have learned. But if what you learned is that God loves prisoners, for example, you might find that the best way of sharing that lesson is to become active in prison ministry. Sharing demonstrates that you don't believe the text is your private possession. It is God's gift to the Christian community.

RESOURCES

The following resources are referenced regularly in the text. In a small group it is a good idea to have different members of the group bring different references. For individual study, use a selection:

1. Study Bibles, with particular reference to *The New Oxford Annotated Bible, New Interpreter's Study Bible, The Harper-Collins Study Bible, The Access Bible,* and *The Today's New International Version (TNIV) Study Bible.* These are not the only Bibles that one might want to consult, and while most of these relate to the NRSV, they do represent a range of versions and viewpoints. You can look

for similar articles in your study Bible. I don't use resources from any one perspective. Look at materials you are likely to disagree with in order to stimulate your thinking. (See Appendix B for information on these resources. The Participatory Bible Study web site, http://www.deepbiblestudy.com, is regularly updated with ideas about materials.

2. Concordances, either English only, or those that include material on the original languages. If you get a concordance, find one that is based on the Bible version you use.

3. Bible Dictionaries, which overlap Study Bibles and Bible Handbooks in terms of their use, but which are very useful for general study of topics you may find.

4. Bible Handbooks, used in much the same way as study Bibles, but without the text of the Bible itself included.

5. Bible Commentaries offer more detailed exegetical explanations and interpretation of the actual text than can be found in the other resources. For the New Testament, I would recommend purchase of *The People's New Testament Commentary* written by Fred Craddock and Eugene Boring.

When it comes to comparing passages you will find your study Bible, concordance, and any Bible with reference notes to be very useful. Remember, however, that even the cross-references are just someone's opinion of how one passage is related to another. You don't have to agree. Look at the passages yourself, and ask not just whether they are related, but *how* they are related.

Remember to keep an open mind and a receptive heart while studying the Bible. Study prayerfully. Meditate on what you read. Try to place yourself in the audience of people who might have first heard this book read to them aloud in a small house church.

COLOSSIANS

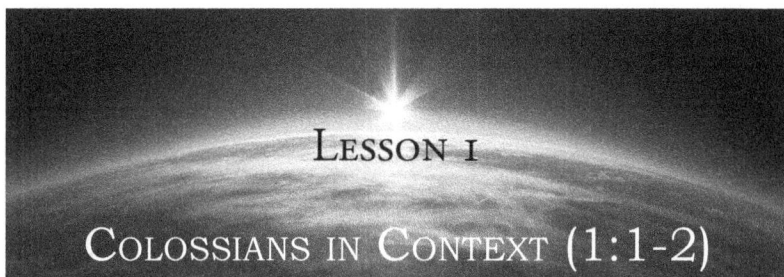

LESSON 1

COLOSSIANS IN CONTEXT (1:1-2)

OBJECTIVE

Lesson one will put the letter to the Colossians into context. The participants will have a basic understanding of the author and his own setting, and the situation of the Colossian Church which occasioned the letter, and a better understanding of the recipients of the letter. In addition, participants will also learn the about the form of letters in the ancient world of the Roman Empire and the Mediterranean world.

OPENING PRAYER

Encounters with God's Word should always start with prayer. It is the Spirit that guides and illumines us as we reflect upon the Scriptures.

God of Revelation, we thank you that you are not a silent God, isolated from humanity, leaving us to guess and speculate about the things that matter.

We pray for those who serve you by studying manuscripts and clarifying texts: for scholars and preachers who wrestle with the words of life for the building up of your Church; for linguists, translators, and publishers who continue to serve the cause of your Gospel by making the Bible available to more and more people.

> *Lord, create in us a hunger for your Word, a thankful-*
> *ness for your Gospel, and a faithfulness to your commands;*
> *through Jesus Christ our Lord. Amen.*[1]

READING: COLOSSIANS 1:1-2

The first thing that should be done in commencing with this study is to read Colossians in its entirety using a version of the Bible, such as the *New Revised Standard Version* or the *New International Version*. You may also use a good translation to compare with the version, such as the *Common English Bible* or the *English Standard Version*. The difference between a version and a translation, generally put, is that a version is a translation done by a team of scholars, while a translation is usually undertaken by one person. Thus, while a version is always a translation, a translation is not necessarily a version.

After reading through Colossians at least once, or more times if you prefer, read an introduction to Colossians in a Bible Dictionary or in a Study Bible. Also look over an outline of the letter provided in your source.

LESSON

AN ANCIENT LETTER

Colossians takes the form of an ancient letter or epistle. In modern letters in the West, the writers identify themselves at the end of the letter. In ancient letters in the Greco-Romans context the authors identify themselves first. After Paul and Timothy identify themselves as the authors, the person(s) being addressed are identified, in this case the members of the church at Colossae.

Then there usually follows a thanksgiving for the recipients of the letter and a reminder as to why the writer is thankful for the them. Then comes the body of the letter which presents the major subject matter that occasioned its writing. This is usually accompa-

---

1   Angela Ashwin (ed.), *The Book of a Thousand Prayers* (Grand Rapids; Zondervan, 2002), p. 53.

nied by exhortation, which is encouragement or a call to some kind of action. Advice is also given on how to handle specific situations faced by the recipients. The letter ends with final greetings and a blessing or benediction.

Letters made their way around the Roman Empire in one of two ways. The Roman army served as the empire's postal service. A letter could be sent by that method. Another way, if it was feasible, was to have a friend or an acquaintance deliver the letter if she or he happened to be traveling in that direction. It appears from Colossians 4:7-8 that this particular epistle was delivered personally by a companion and colleague of Paul, Tychicus. Onesimus, who is the subject of Paul's letter to Philemon, also traveled to Colossae with Tychicus. We will discuss that in more detail when specifically addressing the letter to Philemon.

Who Wrote Colossians?

The writers of the epistle identify themselves as "Paul, an apostle of Jesus Christ by the will of God, and Timothy our brother (1:1)." Scholars have disputed whether the letter comes from St. Paul or from someone writing in the apostle's name after his death. Writing in the name of someone else (called pseudonymity), a respected teacher or leader, was not unheard of in the ancient world. In some quarters it was not necessarily an unacceptable practice, but neither was it universally welcomed. It wasn't until the modern era that the Pauline authorship of Colossians was questioned. It is currently the case that approximately 6 out of 10 New Testament scholars believe that Paul was not the writer.

The reasons for this are several. The style of Colossians is different from the letters scholars universally accept as being from the hand of Paul (Romans, 1 and 2 Corinthians, Galatians, 1 Thessalonians, and Philemon); so too is the vocabulary. In addition, many have noted the differences in theology, which at times seems to have developed beyond the undisputed Pauline letters.

But, while more than a few have found these factors to be compelling in rejecting Paul's authorship, other scholars have not, and neither do I. In his treatment of this matter, John Barclay writes, "If Colossians is by a later Paulinist, it is unparalleled in its sophisticated adaptation of incidental details to camouflage its authenticity"[2]

The theological themes of Colossians and their expression are certainly consistent with Pauline expression. It is true that the vocabulary is different, but it is not as dissimilar as many have proposed. The real difference between Colossians and the accepted Pauline epistles is one of style and that can be explained from the letter itself. Verse 1 of Chapter 1 identifies Paul *and Timothy* as co-authors of the letter. Paul was in jail during the composition of this letter. What if the imprisoned Paul found himself in a situation where he was unable to write or dictate a letter?[3] Paul received word of the problems in Colossae. A response was necessary but he was unable, for whatever reason, to dictate the letter or have first-hand input into its composition. In such a situation Paul would have no option but to trust a companion, familiar with his thinking, to draft a letter after he outlined his general concerns to the one who would pen the letter. If this were indeed what happened (and it cannot be proven nor denied), then it would explain the stylistic, vocabulary, and thematic differences between Colossians and the earlier Pauline letters. It would also account for the Pauline character of the letter.

Thus, Timothy is the actual writer of the epistle with Paul giving it his stamp of approval in 4:18. It could also be that Paul specifically wanted to attend to the matter of Onesimus with Philemon and give his direct attention to that letter while leaving the Colossian correspondence to Timothy.[4] If Philemon was written around the same time as Colossians (which is likely) and given the

---

2   John M.G. Barclay, *Colossians and Philemon,* New Testament
      Guides (Sheffield: Sheffield Academic Press, 1997), p. 24.

3   Where Paul was in prison at the time is a matter of debate. See
      Marianne Meye Thompson, *Colossians and Philemon* (Grand Rap-
      ids: Eerdmans, 2005), pp. 5-6.

4   James D.G. Dunn, *The Epistles to the Colossians and Philemon*
      (Grand Rapids: Eerdmans, 1996), p. 40.

calm tone of Colossians itself, such factors allow us to entertain the possibility.

I, therefore, proceed in this study guide on the assumption that Paul and Timothy are the authors of Colossians

WHAT ABOUT THE CITY OF COLOSSAE?

When Paul and Timothy wrote to the Colossians, the glory days of the city of Colossae were a long and distant memory. In the first century, the Roman philosopher, Pliny the Elder (23-79 AD) referred to Colossae as an insignificant and dwindling city.[5] Its closest neighbors, Laodicea and Hierapolis were larger. The region was known for its wool production. "Colossian wool," as it was known, was dyed dark red in color. The valley in which Colossae was situated also produced great harvests of figs and olives.[6]

Colossae was located in Asia Minor (modern day Turkey) in the Lycus Valley. The region experienced a large earthquake in 60-61 AD. Laodicea was destroyed. One ancient source lists Colossae as fallen, and there is no evidence that Colossae was inhabited after the earthquake until the second century AD.[7] This is significant because it means that Colossians would have to have been written prior to this earthquake. Had Paul and Timothy written it just following the disaster, it would be inconceivable that they would not have mentioned it in their letter.

While Colossae was more of a town and less a city by Paul's day, it would still have had quite a cosmopolitan feel. The population seems to have consisted of native born Phrygians from west central Turkey, and Greek immigrants who had settled in the land generations before. Moreover, in the second century BC, Antiochus III brought approximately two thousand Jewish families from Mesopotamia and Babylon to settle in the area.[8] Jewish influence was

5   *Natural History, Volume II, Books 3-7.*
6   Peter T. O'Brien, *Colossians, Philemon* (Waco: Word, 1982), p. xxvi.
7   Andrew Lincoln, "Colossians," p. 580.
8   Josephus, *Antiquities*, 12. 147-153.

felt in the region along with an amalgam of pagan religious practices. It is this religious context that makes it difficult to diagnose
the problem that Paul and Timothy are addressing in their letter.

WHO WERE THE RECIPIENTS OF THE LETTER?

The letter to the Colossians suggests that the church there
was founded by Epaphras (1:16-17). And while it is possible that
Paul may have passed through Colossae on one of his missionary
journeys, there is no reason to believe that he stayed there for any
length of time because he never visited the church there in person
(2:1). We do not know how large the Christian population was at
Colossae, but it is rather safe to deduce that it did consist of several
house churches. From Philemon 2, we know that a congregation
gathered at his home. Moreover, if I am correct on the major reason for the letter (more on that in the next section), then it would
suggest that the church in that dwindling city was large enough to
be noticed by other groups.

While it cannot be ruled out that there were a minority of Jews
who made up the Colossian church, by and large the Christians
there consisted of Gentiles. Paul employs language in the letter that
clearly indicates this (cf. 1:12, 21, 27; 2:13; 3:5).[9]

WHY WAS THE LETTER WRITTEN?

Perhaps even more controversial than who wrote Colossians
is the reason for its composition. In the past couple of decades,
in particular, much ink has been spilled in addressing this matter.
While it is not possible to delve too much into detail on the exact
character of what I refer to as "the Colossian philosophy" that
Paul and Timothy are warning against (2:8), the options must be
generally delineated.

The ancient world was just as religiously diverse as the modern
one. We who live in the world of space travel and high technology
like to consider ourselves much more advanced than our more

9   Douglas J. Moo, *The Letters to the Colossians and to Philemon*
     (Grand Rapids: Eerdmans, 2008), pp. 27-28.

primitive forbearers. But the truth of the matter is that for every type and brand and shape of modern religious belief currently in existence, one can find a parallel in the ancient world as well. The world of Paul and Timothy was just as religiously diverse as our own and the options before us were also in front of them.

In general, scholars have offered two major possibilities on the problem that Paul and Timothy are targeting in their letter. A few other suggestions have been made by a small minority of scholars, but their arguments have largely not been embraced.

The first option is that the Colossian philosophy contained a mixture of religious practices or a religious syncretism has been suggested by many scholars. This mixture included everything from Greek philosophical beliefs, appeals to magic and incantations, popular folk religion, and a small amount of Jewish practice all mixed together. Scholars who promote the syncretistic thesis disagree on what are the most significant elements of the mixture or whether even certain components are present. Nevertheless, if this first option is correct, then there appears to be some pressure coming from a group within the church, or from the outside, to incorporate these syncretistic elements into the Christianity of the Colossian believers.

The second option, which I favor, is that the character of the Colossian philosophy is basically Jewish in nature and that the proponents of the philosophy are Jews from the synagogue in town who are promoting their Judaism to the church and arguing that the Colossian Christians have distorted the ancestral faith they have embraced by not incorporating certain Jewish practices in their life and worship (Colossians 2:8, 11, 16-18). It may also be that there is a group (of Jewish Christians?) from within the church promoting this philosophy.[10] Thus, Paul and Timothy write to warn the Christians of the dangers of doing so. The tone of the letter is quite calm, suggesting that the Christians have not embraced the practices of

10   An option preferred by Ben Witherington III, *The Letters to Philemon, the Colossians, and the Ephesians* (Grand Rapids: Eerdmans, 2007), p. 164.

the synagogue, but may be entertaining the possibility. This is to be contrasted with Paul's letter to the Galatians where the Christians have already incorporated such practices into their life and worship. Such an already accomplished amalgamation would explain Paul's extremely angry tone and harsh language in that letter.[11] As we move throughout this commentary I will highlight, when appropriate, the Jewish character of the Colossian philosophy and the writers' response to it.

OPENING GREETING (1:1-2)

Several noteworthy details are found already in the first two verses of Colossians. First, the Apostle Paul describes himself as "an apostle of Christ Jesus by the will of God." The Greek word *apostolos* means "sent one." Here Paul is using it specifically to refer to himself who was called in special fashion by Jesus Christ to join in the work of the twelve original disciples Jesus called to a unique status. But elsewhere, he uses it in a broader sense to refer to those who are involved in the mission of the gospel (1 Thessalonians 2:6-7).

In referring to himself in this way and reminding his hearers that he is an apostle by the will of God, Paul is bolstering his credentials, which some in other contexts had been considered suspect (Galatians 1:11-2:10).

The recipients of the letter are referred to as "saints and faithful brothers (and sisters)." Paul characteristically uses the term "saints" in his letters to designate the Christians to whom he is writing (Romans 1:7; 1 Corinthians 1:2; 2 Corinthians 1:1; Philippians 1:1; Ephesians 1:1). A saint is "a holy one" (Greek *hagios*; Latin *sanctus*, from where we get our word "sanctification"), whom God has set apart for a specific purpose. In referring to the Colossian Christians as saints, Paul is reminding them that they too are called by the will of God for God's purposes. And in referring to the Colossian

---

11   See Allan R. Bevere, *Sharing in the Inheritance: Identity and the Moral Life in Colossians* (Sheffield: Sheffield Academic Press, 2003), pp. 58-59.

saints as "faithful," Paul affirms that the Colossians have kept their charge well. This fits the calm tone of the letter, suggesting that whatever the Colossians are facing, it has not infiltrated into the church as of yet.

Finally, Paul and Timothy conclude their greeting with a wish of "grace and peace from God our Father." To offer a greeting of grace is typical of Paul and signifies that the Colossians' status as faithful saints is a result of the gracious initiative of God and that they are members of the new covenant because of what God the Father has done for them through his Son, Jesus Christ. "Peace" (Greek *eirēnē*) carries with it the Jewish concept of the Hebrew word, *shalom*, which is a wish for one's well-being in all areas of life.

DISCUSSION QUESTIONS

1. The original recipients of this letter would have heard the letter read aloud as a gathered congregation. Making copies of written material in the ancient world was time consuming and expensive. The Colossians would not have had the luxury of sitting down with the words of this letter in front of them to analyze and reflect on like we do today. How different would it be to hear these words instead of reading them? What advantages do we have in being able to sit with the letter to the Colossians in front of us? What advantages might the Colossians have had over us in having to listen to Paul's words?

2. We have tended to reserve the word "Apostle" to refer only to the original twelve disciples and St. Paul, and rightly so. But there is a sense in which all Christians are "apostles" with a little "a" in that we are all sent by Jesus Christ to bear witness to the Good News. In what ways can we answer our calling as ones who are sent by Jesus Christ to the gathered community of saints, to our families, friends, workplace and social gatherings?

3. Paul refers to the Colossians as "saints." Who are the saints, "the holy ones," in your life that have had a formative effect on your faith?

4.   The early Christians lived in a religiously diverse world just as we do today. How can we live and model the Good News of Jesus Christ as God's way to salvation and also exercise tolerance and even friendship to those around us who believe differently?

EXERCISE

Read through Colossians at least three times. Write down questions you would like to ask about the letter for further discussion.

As you reflect upon the saints in your life, let them know of their importance in your faith journey. Send them an email or give them a phone call. If possible, set up a time to meet with one of your saints personally to let them know face-to-face how much they have meant to you.

HISTORICAL/THEOLOGICAL REFLECTION

It is clear from the writings that the Apostle Paul considered his call as the foundation of his ministry. It was his calling that formed his way of life. As Paul reminds the Colossians that they are saints, meaning they have been called and set apart for God's purposes, so we saints today are also called by God for his purposes in this world. Please consider the following words from Oswald Chambers:

> Paul states here that the call of God is to preach the gospel. But remember what Paul means by "the gospel," namely, the reality of redemption in our Lord Jesus Christ. We are inclined to make sanctification the goal of our preaching. Paul refers to personal experiences only by way of illustration, never as the end of the matter. We are not commissioned to preach salvation or sanctification—we are commissioned to lift up Jesus Christ (see John 12:32). It is an injustice to say that Jesus Christ labored in redemption to make me a saint. Jesus Christ labored in redemption to redeem the whole world and to place it perfectly whole and restored before the throne of God. The fact that we can experience redemption illustrates the power of

its reality, but that experience is a byproduct and not the goal of redemption. If God were human, how sick and tired He would be of the constant requests we make for our salvation and for our sanctification. We burden His energies from morning till night asking for things for ourselves or for something from which we want to be delivered! When we finally touch the underlying foundation of the reality of the gospel of God, we will never bother Him anymore with little personal complaints.

The one passion of Paul's life was to proclaim the gospel of God. He welcomed heartbreak, disillusionment, and tribulation for only one reason— these things kept him unmovable in his devotion to the gospel of God.[12]

Closing Prayer

As this first lesson comes to a close, use the following prayer as a guide to our entire journey through Colossians and Philemon.

Illumine our hearts; O Master Who loves mankind, with the pure light of Thy divine knowledge. Open the eyes of our mind to the understanding of your gospel teachings.

Implant also in us the fear of your blessed commandments, that trampling down all carnal desires, we may enter upon a spiritual manner of living, both thinking and doing such things as are well-pleasing to you.

For You are the illumination of our souls and bodies, O Christ our God, and to You we ascribe glory, together with Your Father, who is from everlasting, and Your all-holy, good, and life-creating Spirit, now and ever and unto ages of ages. Amen.[13]

---

12 "The Call of God," http://utmost.org/the-call-of-god/.
13 Orthodox Church of the Holy Cross, Medford, NJ. http://www.holycrossmedford.org/.

LESSON 2
THANKING GOD FOR FAITHFUL SAINTS
(1:3-14)

OBJECTIVE

In lesson two we will focus upon the significance of thanksgiving—thanksgiving to God for who God is and what God has accomplished, and the necessity of being thankful for fellow Christians whom he has called to be in mission with us. Participants will learn that gratitude is the necessary posture for the believer in all of life. It allows Christians to reach out to others in a sacrificial way, knowing that they can do so because Jesus Christ has offered himself for everyone on the cross. In gratitude for Christ's work, the church continues his sacrificial work in the world. Readers will also be encouraged to be thankful for God's people Israel, through whom the offer of universal salvation has come.

OPENING PRAYER

As we begin lesson two let us thank God for God's calling of women and men to missions across the world, especially those who face hardships for the sake of their calling.

> *Eternal father, it is your joy to call men and women to serve you across the barriers of race and language and culture: Give them strength and courage, and satisfy their longing to make known the good news of Christ.*
>
> *Bless those who are called along the humble road, to serve and support but not to lead.*
>
> *When they face danger, save them from fear,*

When they are disheartened, be their friend;

When they think they have failed, show them the
cross.

> *Give them peace in their hearts,*
> *and peace in their homes,*
> *and the joy of acceptance by those whom they serve.*

For Jesus Christ's sake.[14]

READING COLOSSIANS 1:3-14

Read 1:3-14 through three times in your preferred translation or version. Then read it again three more times in a translation that is more conceptual (and less formal) in character such as *The Message* or *The Common English Bible*.

LESSON

THANKFULNESS FOR ALL THE SAINTS

Colossians 1:3-8 is one sentence in Greek. Most translations divide the passage into several sentences to make it more readable. To begin a letter with thanksgiving was common in ancient letters, whether Roman, Greek, or Jewish. In all of Paul's undisputed letters, except for Galatians, he offers thanksgiving to God for the recipients.

Paul and Timothy always thank God the Father of the Lord Jesus Christ when they pray for the Colossians. It is important to note that nowhere in the Apostle's writings does he directly thank the recipients of his letters; he thanks God for the recipients. This is quite different from our normal practice in the modern West where we directly thank one another for services rendered or for a gift. But Paul thanks God for the Colossians' faith in Christ Jesus and the love they have for the saints. God is the source of the good

---

14   Angela Ashwin (ed.), *The Book of a Thousand Prayers* (Grand Rapids; Zondervan, 2002), p. 447.

gifts for which Paul is thankful including the saints at Colossae themselves. [15]

Moreover, there is a Christ-centered quality to Paul's thankfulness. As we shall see Jesus plays a central and prominent role in Colossians, which may suggest to us something of the dilemma Paul and Timothy are addressing in the letter. The Colossians' faith in Christ and the fruit it has produced has come to them because other faithful saints brought it to them. Fruit produces more fruit.

THANKFULNESS TO GOD AND FOR THE WORK OF JESUS CHRIST

Paul and Timothy move from their thankfulness for the Colossian Christians to a reminder of their continual prayers for them. It is important to note that their prayers for the Colossians are persistent.

Moreover, their prayers for the Colossians are specific: "... asking that you may be filled with the knowledge of God's will in all spiritual wisdom and understanding, so that you may lead lives worthy of the Lord, fully pleasing to him, as you bear fruit in every good work and as you grow in the knowledge of God" (1:9-10). In ancient Judaism the knowledge of God's will is known through the Law of Moses (e.g. Romans 2:17-20; Baruch 3:24-4:4; Sirach 24:23). Such knowledge is to be had through "spiritual wisdom and understanding."

According to the Greek philosopher Aristotle, wisdom and understanding are two of the three principal intellectual virtues. Unlike what Aristotle called "the moral virtues" which were acquired through education, he believed that the intellectual virtues were given by a combination of nature and nurture, that is, while such virtues could be strengthened through experience and education, it was necessary that a person be given them by "natural endowments" (*Nicomachean Ethics*, 1143b 8-9; Aristotle will contradict himself on this later in his *Ethics*).

---

15   Marianne Meye Thompson, *Colossians and Philemon* (Grand Rapids: Eerdmans, 2005), p. 190.

Paul and Timothy, however, appear to have a more Jewish and biblical understanding in mind. Wisdom and understanding are not given by nature, but are received as divine gifts. Thus, the writers can pray and ask God to grant these virtues to the Christians at Colossae. Even though such virtues are divinely received, they can also be nurtured as one travels with Christ and his church along the way. Paul prays that the Colossians may "filled with the knowledge of God's will." Such filling suggests movement toward a completed or finished state. Spiritual growth is in mind here. So while knowledge revealed through spiritual wisdom and understanding are divinely given, the believer plays an important role in cooperation in nurturing those gifts.

Such knowledge "suggests the ability to discern the truth and to make good decisions based on that truth."[16] This knowledge is necessary if the Christians at Colossae are to "bear fruit in every good work." Once again we see the Jewish character of this letter. The imagery of bearing fruit in one's life is found throughout ancient Jewish literature, particularly in the prophets of the Old Testament (e.g. Isaiah 37:31; Jeremiah 17:8; Ezekiel 17:23).

The authors are not interested in divine knowledge for its own sake. Rather, it is to aid the Colossians in their life together as the church. The gospel is credible only as it is demonstrated by individual saints and the church collectively in the good works that bear witness to God's kingdom. Christian convictions must be revealed in practice (cf. James 2:18). If one is to live in God's world and bear fruit, one must have knowledge of God's will in wisdom and understanding.

From thankfulness to unceasing prayer, Paul and Timothy move to express their hope for the Colossians—that they may be made strong in divine strength and that they may be prepared to endure all things with patience and giving thanks to God in the midst of it all (vv. 11-12a). The Colossians have this hope because they are "a people in whose life the new age has already dawned"

---

16   Douglas J. Moo, *The Letters to the Colossians and to Philemon* (Grand Rapids: Eerdmans, 2008), p. 94.

(compare Galatians 5:22-23), with the capacity to maintain hope in God's future triumph (Colossians 1:5; 1 Thessalonians 5:14) even in the midst of present adversity (2 Corinthians 6:4; James 1:2-4; 5:10-11).[17]

The Colossians can be confident of having such strength and patience because in verses 12-14 he clearly connects the church as God's chosen people in continuity with God's chosen Israel. Paul employs echoes of the Old Testament in these verses—echoes that hearken back to the Exodus from Egypt and Israel's entrance into the Promised Land of Canaan—deliverance and sharing in the inheritance (cf. Deuteronomy 10:9; 12:12; 14:27, 29; 18:1; Joshua 19:9; Jeremiah 13:25). Paul and Timothy appropriate this imagery and use it in reference to the church, which includes both Jews and Gentiles. The Gentile Christians now share in the inheritance of deliverance and salvation given to Israel by God's grace. The affirmation of 1:12-14 (cf. Ephesians 2:11-13) implies that the inheritance of the people of God given by grace is no longer the privilege of one race, but has now been expanded to include those not of Jewish background. "The promise of the land is widened into the promise of a whole new creation."[18]

EXODUS: THANKFULNESS FOR THE LIBERATION OF GOD'S PEOPLE ISRAEL

N.T. Wright notes that God's wisdom is active in the world. It is expressed in the Torah (Law of Moses), and it has made its home in Israel.[19] Israel's employment of wisdom as embodied in Torah continued to affirm its uniqueness from the other nations of the world. To claim that the wisdom of the one true God was actualized in Torah was also to claim a special place for the people

---

17   Robert W. Wall, *Colossians and Philemon* (Downers: Grove: Inter-Varsity Press, 1993), pp. 53-54.

18   N.T. Wright, *Colossians and Philemon*, Tyndale New Testament Commentaries (Downers Give: IVP Academic, 2008, p. 61.

19   N.T. Wright *Climax of the Covenant: Christ and the Law in Pauline Theology* (Minneapolis: Fortress Press, 1991), p. 110.

of that one true God. In asserting that Jesus embodies God's wisdom, the authors of Colossians (Paul and Timothy) were making a unique claim as well in reference to the people who believed in Jesus, whether Jew or Gentile.

Similarly, the continued telling and retelling of the story of the Exodus from Egypt was meant for deeper purposes than entertainment and simple reminder. The stories of Israel's deliverance also signified the special place of Israel as the people of God. In addition, it would be a reminder of the deliverance yet to come. Thus Paul and Timothy use the Exodus "echoes" as a way of explicating the work of Christ as the final liberation from slavery.

The clearest reminder of the Exodus and the uniqueness of the people of God is to be found early in Colossians in 1:12-14. In 1:12 Paul and Timothy give thanks to God the Father "who has enabled you to share in the inheritance of the saints in the light." The authors addressing the Gentile Christians in this very Jewish way, reaffirm what the Colossians must have been told when the gospel was first preached to them: they have a share in the inheritance of God's people. The Greek words for "share" and "inheritance" in verse 12 are often found together in the Septuagint (see Deuteronomy 10:9; 12:12; 14:27, 29; 18:1; Joshua 19:9; Jeremiah 13:25). Because of their faith in Christ they "share in the inheritance of God's gracious gift of the land of Canaan to Israel."[20]

The authors appropriate this image and use it in reference to the church, which includes both Jews and Gentiles. The Gentiles now share in the inheritance given to Israel by God's grace. They are to be numbered among those who are called "saints." Some commentators have suggested that the phrase "of the saints in the light" refers to angels, as the authors are arguing in opposition to a cult of angels in the Colossian church.[21] But it is not necessary

---

20   Eduard Schweizer, *Letter to the Colossians* (Minneapolis: Augsburg, 1982), p. 50.

21   e.g. Troy Martin, *By Philosophy and Empty Deceit: Colossians as a Response to a Cynic Critique* (Sheffield: Sheffield Academic Press, 1996), p. 54.

to believe that the Colossian Christians were involved in angel worship. Moreover, the Greek term for "holy" in Pauline literature normally refers to the followers of Jesus. This is certainly the meaning of the word in Colossian 1:1. Unless there is specific evidence that the authors are shifting the meaning of the same word, it is best to understand "saints" in 1:12 as a reference to Christians, who in worship share a foretaste of heaven.

The affirmation of 1:12 implies that the inheritance of the people of God given by grace is no longer the privilege of one race, but now has expanded to include those not of Jewish background. To quote N.T. Wright, "The promise of the land is widened into the promise of a whole new creation."[22]

The Exodus theme in Colossians is intensified in 1:13 with the phrase, "into the Kingdom of his beloved Son," which is reminiscent of Israel as God's son called out of slavery in Egypt (Hosea 11:1). Such imagery in this prayer is entirely appropriate as Paul and Timothy then move into a hymn about the Lordship of Christ (1:15-20). It is in Christ that God's people are liberated and freed from the powers that enslaved them. They now share in the bounty brought by the new covenant.

This language in 1:12-14 sets the stage for the Christ-hymn as it casts Jesus in these roles. The word "firstborn," for example, is used in the Septuagint (the Greek translation of the Hebrew Old Testament, translated in the third century B.C. and hereafter will be abbreviated "LXX") to denote a special relationship between a father and his son. In Exodus 4:22 Israel is referred to as "my first-born son," signifying God's special relationship with the Hebrews (reminiscent of Jesus' baptism, cf. Matthew 2:15). In addition, the patriarchs, the Torah, and the messianic king are referred to in this way, denoting a special relationship to God. Psalm 88:27 (LXX) states about this messianic king: "I will make him my firstborn, higher than the kings of the earth." Firstborn emphasizes uniqueness. The firstborn is to be distinguished from the rest of creation.

---

22   N.T. Wright, *Colossians and Philemon,* Tyndale New Testament Commentaries (Downers Give: IVP Academic, 2008, 61.

The firstborn of all creation (1:15), Christ is unique and to be demarcated from creation. As the agent of creation Christ is superior. By virtue of his agency in creation (another theme found in Jewish literature, cf. Psalm 104:24), Christ has dominion over all things.

There is little doubt that Colossians 1:12-14 would have elicited in its reader's thoughts of the Exodus. Thus Christ's work of reconciliation in the hymn (Colossians 1:15-20) and reflected in Torah (see Sirach 1:1-10; 24:3-12) has now made her home in Christ. As wisdom reflects the image of God's goodness (Wisdom of Solomon 7:26), so Christ reflects the image of the invisible God (Colossians 1:15).

In the Colossian Christ-hymn the Jewish notions of wisdom, Torah, and Israel are linked together in order to argue that Christ is all-sufficient for the Colossians. The major argument put forth in Colossians is that Christ is sufficient for Christian faith and practice. The Colossians need not look elsewhere.

Wisdom, Torah, and Exodus are themes intrinsic to Israel's self-understanding, and they are used to remind the Colossians that as they started their journey as God's people in Christ, they can and must continue their journey as God's people in Christ. As people in Christ they can "bear fruit (a Jewish notion) in every good work" (Colossians 1:10; cf. Jeremiah 1:9-10; 18:7-9; 24:6; 31:28; 42:10). Nothing else needs to be accomplished.

While Paul and Timothy will insist that the Colossian Christians need not conform to observing Torah regulations, they must nevertheless be thankful to God for God's people Israel through whom the Savior, Jesus Christ has come, who now offers salvation to all. The promises of God are not reserved exclusively for Israel, but they come through Israel. That is a blessing for all.

DISCUSSION QUESTIONS

1. It had been noted that Paul never directly thanks the Colossians or any of the saints in his other letters directly (I thank you), but instead he thanks God for them. Should this change the

way we offer our appreciation to our fellow saints in the church for their ministries? What do you think?

2. Knowing that God is the one who gives us divine knowledge and spiritual wisdom and understanding, how can believers nurture such knowledge as we travel on our faith journey? How can our fellow saints assist us in such spiritual growth?

3. Paul and Timothy are very clear in verses 12-14—the deliverance and the inheritance of salvation are now open to all people. In Ephesians, Paul states that Jesus Christ has torn down the dividing wall of hostility between Jews and Gentiles (2:11-22). What dividing walls do we Christians continue to build keeping people away from receiving the Good News of Jesus?

4. Paul and Timothy pray unceasingly for the Colossians. Jesus also tells us to be unrelenting in our prayers (Luke 18:1-7). Why should we be persistent in our prayers? Isn't it enough to mention our concerns once to God? What do you think?

EXERCISE

Read through Colossians 1:3-14 at least three times. Write down questions you would like to ask about the letter for further discussion.

In the next week write or send an email to three persons you know who volunteer their time for the church. Instead of thanking them directly for their faithfulness tell them in the note that you thank God for them and that you pray for them. (If you haven't been, please start doing so.)

HISTORICAL/THEOLOGICAL REFLECTION

Enda McDonagh writes that prayer is the way we let God loose in the world.[23] Theologian and ethicist, Stanley Hauerwas connects the power of prayer to the sacraments:

---

23   Enda McDonagh, *Doing the Truth: The Quest for Moral Theology* (Notre Dame: University of Notre Dame Press, 1979), pp. 40-57.

Baptism and Eucharist are our most fervent prayers and set the standard for all of our prayers. For prayer is not our pleading to an unmovable or unsympathetic, but all-powerful God. Rather it is through prayer that we learn to make ourselves open to God's presence.... Prayer, therefore, though a common activity, is a dangerous one, for God's presence is not easily controlled. God is a wild presence calling us to ways of life we had not imagined possible. Through baptism and the Eucharist, the Christian people open themselves to that wildness. It is no wonder that if possible the rulers would prevent Christians from praying, since there is no more powerful challenge to their power.[24]

CLOSING PRAYER

The Old Testament is very clear. Moses did not lead the people out of slavery in Egypt; it was God. Moses was only God's human instrument. The psalmist declares that God delivered Israel "with a mighty hand and an outstretched arm (Psalm 136, especially v. 12). True freedom and deliverance can only come from God.

O God, our Rescuer and our Redeemer, you led your people out of slavery and darkness into your own freedom and light. You make a covenant with us in the waters of baptism and call us to continue our pilgrimage, following the Lord Jesus on his way of the cross to new and eternal life. Help us to persevere on this journey, trusting in your continual guidance and endless love, through Jesus Christ our Lord. Amen.[25]

---

24 Stanley Hauerwas, *The Peaceable Kingdom: A Primer in Christian Ethics* (Notre Dame: University of Notre Dame Press, 1986), p. 108.

25 Hoyt Hickman, et al, Handbook of the Christian Year (Nashville: Abingdon Press, 1989), p. 217.

LESSON 3

THE COSMIC CHRIST (1:15-23)

OBJECTIVE

Lesson three will highlight the singular significance of Jesus Christ in God's plan for salvation and the indispensable role he plays in the reconciliation of all things to God. Moreover, readers will gain an appreciation for the emphasis on Christ as the very incarnation of God. In addition, participants will focus on the importance of the church and its place in the reconciling mission of Jesus Christ in the world. The work of Jesus Christ in cross and resurrection make reconciliation possible. The church is the vehicle by which that reconciliation is offered and embodied. The church is to be the incarnation of Christ to the world.

OPENING PRAYER

Jesus Christ is the redeemer of the world and God's people the church are to bear witness to that salvation in word and deed. Let us offer this prayer from the Church in Korea.

> *Almighty God, our Father, you have redeemed us by the death and resurrection of your only Son Jesus Christ and given us your Holy Spirit that we may be your witnesses in the world: banish the powers of darkness and sin from the minds of those who refuse to believe in your name and open their hearts to your gospel that they may believe in you and become temples of your Holy Spirit. Grant also that we who believe in you may be effective ministers of your Word to those whose lives have not been touched by your saving grace. We*

*make this prayer through our Lord Jesus Christ who reigns
with you and the Holy Spirit, one God for ever and ever.*[26]

READING COLOSSIANS 1:15-23

Read Colossians 1:15-23 through several times. Write down
five words that you believe are significant in the passage. Prepare
to answer why you believe they are important after this lesson has
been completed.

LESSON

INTRODUCTION

New Testament scholars generally agree that Colossians 1:15-
20 is a hymn or a poem written in the early decades of Christianity
and was likely used in worship. Some have suggested that the Apostle Paul wrote the hymn himself,[27] while others believe that Paul
was utilizing an earlier composition that was known by the Colossians and incorporated it into his letter as a way to persuade the
Christians of the city, though Paul may have edited it somewhat
to suit his purposes.[28] This hymn reveals that the writer had, what
scholars referred to as a "high Christology," that is, a view of Jesus
which emphasized his divinity. It was the fourth century bishop,
Athanasius who argued that Jesus must be divine, otherwise it
would not be proper to refer to him as Savior, since only God can
save. The Colossian Christ-Hymn reflects both Jesus as in the "image of the invisible God," and as the one who reconciles all things.

---

26   *The Complete Book of Christian Prayer* (New York: Continuum,
     1995), p. 402.

27   e.g. Kümmel, *Introduction to the New Testament*, pp. 342-
     343.

28   Ben Witherington III, *The Letters to Philemon, the Colossians, and
     the Ephesians* (Grand Rapids: Eerdmans, 2007), pp. 130-131.

Incarnational Christology

Tom Wright correctly argues that the Christ-Hymn should be understood in the context of what he refers to as "mainline Judaism,"[29] that is, it reflects a Jewish worldview. It is this Jewish character of the hymn that makes the hymn intelligible in the context of the letter to the Colossians. Several important terms present in this passage help us to understand what Paul believes about Christ and his cosmic work.

Wisdom—Wisdom played a very important role in the theology of Jesus' day. Wisdom had come to be identified with Torah. The Torah was believed to be the very wisdom of God.[30] Wisdom is also a significant theme found in some of the Dead Sea Scrolls. In analyzing 1:15-20 it appears the theme that holds the Christ-Hymn together is the notion of wisdom. The apocryphal book, Wisdom of Solomon 7:26 reads, "For she is a reflection of eternal light, a spotless mirror of the working of God, and an image of his goodness," which is reminiscent of Colossians 1:15. In ancient Jewish literature wisdom was closely associated with creation (e.g. Proverbs 8:22). Drawing on the place of wisdom in the act of creation, Paul seems to suggest that Christ is that wisdom present at the beginning. One author notes, "The Old Testament portrait of wisdom bears a "striking resemblance to the Christ described by Paul."[31]

Wisdom is not only present at the creation of the universe, but it provides knowledge for living in the ways of God. Proverbs 8:35-36 states, "The one who finds me finds life, and obtains favor from the Lord. But the one who sins against me injures himself; all those who hate me love death." In Colossians Paul is presenting Christ as the wisdom of God, present at creation and offering redemption.

29　N.T. Wright, *Climax of the Covenant: Christ and the Law in Pauline Theology* (Minneapolis: Fortress Press, 1991), p. 107.

30　See George W.E. Nickelsburg, *Jewish Literature Between the Bible and the Mishnah* (Philadelphia: Fortress Press, 1991), pp. 59-62.

31　W.D. Davies, *Paul and Rabbinic Judaism: Some Rabbinic elements in Pauline Theology* (London: SPCK, 1958), p. 151.

If ancient Jews believed that the Torah was God's wisdom embodied, what are the implications then of Christ as God's wisdom embodied? Quite simply Paul is conferring upon Christ everything previously applied to wisdom which was embodied in the Torah. As the Law of Moses was sufficient for the life of the people of Israel because it was God's wisdom embodied, so Jesus was sufficient for the faith and practice of the people of God, the church, because Christ was God's wisdom embodied.

First-Born—What does it mean that Jesus is the first-born of all creation? It refers to Jesus as the Savior of the world as one who has priority over all creation. The purpose of the world and the universe is found in Jesus Christ. Christ has supremacy over all of creation because he is the first-born "from the dead." He is the first installment of the future resurrection of his people.

First-born should not be interpreted that somehow the Son, the second member of the Trinity was created. Trinitarian theology holds that the Son is eternal and not a created being. First-born emphasizes Jesus' priority of place as the resurrected Lord of creation.

Thrones, dominions, rulers, and powers—As first-born Christ is supreme over all of creation, including natural and supernatural powers. In Jewish literature, the words translated "thrones" and "dominions" are sometime designated among the multitude of angels. The word for "rulers" is used to refer to earthly and spiritual authorities, while the word translated "powers" likely denotes earthly rulers. So, Paul and Timothy probably have in mind both and spiritual and earthly authorities. Indeed, the Bible does suggest that the earthly nations are under the direction of spiritual forces (Luke 4:5-7).

The question is whether or not the authors have only evil forces in mind or both malevolent and benevolent. Colossians 1:13 suggests that they are threatening, yet the context of the Christ-hymn is that Christ is head over all the principalities and powers were created "in the heavens and on the earth" (1:16). Thus both hostile and amicable forces are probably in mind. If part of the problem with the Colossian philosophy the writers are confronting is the practice of worshiping the angels as well as worshiping with them, then Paul's point that Jesus is superior to all heavenly beings, including the angels is particularly important. Thus, right from the earliest stage of this letter, Paul and Timothy prepare to make the point that Christ has defeated and is, therefore, superior to the hostile forces (2:15), and he is superior to the angelic powers that the Colossian philosophers find so intriguing.[32]

Fullness—In 1:19, Paul and Timothy write, "For in him [Christ] all the fullness of God was pleased to dwell." In the Old Testament the fullness of God's presence means that God is imminent and closely involved in the world. (Psalms 72:19; Jeremiah 23:24; Ezekiel 43:5; 44:4), and creation itself reflects the fullness of God's glory (Psalms 24:1). It also refers to completeness.

In addition, the word translated "pleasure" refers to the idea of God's good pleasure in the divine election of his people (Psalms 44:3; 147:11; 149:4). In the context of Colossians this refers specifically to God's unique revelation in Jesus Christ who is also the elected one. Jesus Christ is truly the incarnation of God.

INCARNATIONAL ECCLESIOLOGY

As Jesus embodies the image of the invisible God, so the church embodies the image of Jesus. "He is the head of the body, the church" (1:18). It is important to note that Paul repeats some of the same language using the same or similar terminology in Christ's relationship to the church as he has just utilized in describing Christ's relationship to creation. The cosmic significance of Jesus Christ is not affirmed here, but the universal importance of the church is emphasized. As Jesus is the incarnation of God, so the church is to incarnate — embody — Christ for the world. The emphasis here is missional. John Chrysostom states,

---

32   Allan R. Bevere, *Sharing in the Inheritance: Identity and the Moral Life in Colossians* (Sheffield: Sheffield Academic Press, 2003), p. 130.

Then having spoken of his dignity [Paul] also proceeds to speak of his love for humanity. "He is," he says, "the head of the body, the church." He did not say "of the fullness of the universe," (although this too is signified) out of a wish to show his great friendliness to us, in that he who is thus above, and above all, connected himself with those below.[33]

The mission is nothing less than the reconciliation of all things. It is Christ who accomplishes the work of reconciliation by the "blood of his cross" (1:20), but the church is the vehicle by which that reconciliation is made known to the world. In its life the church is to bear witness to that reconciliation in word and in deed; the reconciliation of the cross is being affected in the church.

DISCUSSION QUESTIONS

1. The earliest Christians sang songs in their worship. The several places in the New Testament where we believe that an early hymn of the church is utilized all focus centrally on Jesus Christ. What does that suggest about the significance of Jesus in early Christian faith and worship?
2. The writers of Colossians have a special place for the church in the work of God in the world. What makes the church unique from all other organizations, religious or otherwise?
3. Christians often think of salvation as something that God only does for individuals, but Colossians is very clear that salvation, reconciliation is a much larger more cosmic thing. Christ will reconcile all things. Have you ever thought about the salvation given by Jesus as something much larger than the concern for human souls? If not, why not?
4. Both John Wesley and C.S. Lewis suggested the restoration of all things would include the animal kingdom because the animals have had to endure the suffering and frailty of a fallen

---

33   Homilies on Colossians 3, Quote in Peter Gorday, ed. *Colossians, 1-2 Thessalonians, 1-2 Timothy, Titus, Philemon*. Ancient Christian Commentary on Scripture IX (Downers Grove: InterVarsity Press, 2000), p. 17.

creation even though they were not responsible for it. Wesley believed that a just God would allow them to participate in the redemption of the world. In other words, they believed that animals would participate in God's salvation. What do you think of this?

Exercise

Of all the words used to describe Christ in 1:15-20, which word means the most to you and why?

Spend some time reflecting on what it means for the church to be the Body of Christ. How does the church reflect the character of Christ in the world? Write down several one word descriptions that depict the church as Christ's presence in this world.

Historical/Theological Reflection

The Nicene Creed, which was the product of the First Council of Nicaea in 325 A.D., states the following about Christ:

> We believe in one Lord, Jesus Christ, the only Son of God, eternally begotten of the Father, God from God, Light from Light, true God from true God, begotten, not made, of one Being with the Father. Through him all things were made. For us and for our salvation he came down from heaven: by the power of the Holy Spirit he became incarnate from the Virgin Mary, and was made man.

Since we often see humanity and deity as two utterly separate things we tend to view them in tension with each other wondering how both deity and humanity can somehow have dwelt in Jesus Christ. But one of the greatest theologians of the twentieth century, Karl Barth, saw them as complimentary. Indeed, he believed it was impossible to have one without the other. He writes in his book *The Humanity of God*, "What is the humanity of God? It is God dealing with humanity. It is wrapped up in his deity. God's deity cannot be properly understood without his humanity. The whole of God's activity toward women and men is his humanity."[34]

In Jesus, humanity and divinity come together in inseparable fashion. Peter Marty states,

> In Bibles that provide chapter headings, this section of Colossians may be titled "The Supremacy of Christ," or something similar. This is the Christ in whom "all the fullness of God was pleased to dwell." Nothing of God is held back or left out of the person of Jesus. Though God once was content to dwell in *places* like Sinai, Zion or the Temple, now God is in a *person*. Everything that God is, and cares about, now resides in Jesus Christ. Christ is the face or the image of the invisible God.[35]

Closing Prayer

Colossians 1:15-20 is often read on Christ the King Sunday that falls every year in November. This is appropriate as the Colossians Christ-Hymn presents Jesus as the Lord of all things. He is indeed the King of Kings.

> *As the shepherd who cares for the flock, O God, you guide all things through Jesus whom you have exalted over all creation as king. Hear the prayers we offer in his name for the creation he cherished and that you entrust to us.*
>
> *Look upon your people who rejoice in your justice and mercy, and grant that the prayers we make may reveal Christ's reign in our time. Amen.*[36]

---

34   Quoted from Allan R. Bevere, "Being Human Is Not the Problem." http://www.allanbevere.com/2013/04/being-human-is-not-problem.html.

35   "Super Glue: Colossians 1:15-20," *The Christian Century*, Vol. 121, No. 23 (November 16, 2004, p. 20.

36   *The Revised Common Lectionary*, Vanderbilt University, http://lectionary.library.vanderbilt.edu/prayers.php?id=290.

OBJECTIVE

In this lesson we will focus on the call and testimony of the Apostle Paul and on the Christians in the church at Colossae. Participants will gain a greater appreciation for the call of God on their lives and the significance of example as testimony to the credibility and truth of the gospel of Jesus Christ. Moreover, growth in discipleship must be understood as a life-long pursuit. Christians must "be rooted and built up in Christ and established in the faith" (2:7). This does not happen instantaneously, nor do we reach a point in this life where believers can say they are finished growing in God's grace.

OPENING PRAYER

Paul reminds the Corinthians that God's people are clay in the divine potter's hands to be fashioned after the will of the Creator (Romans 9:21; see Jeremiah 18:1-11). It is God who calls; we simply answer. We must be willing to allow God to make us into his vessels for his purposes in this world. Let this prayer from the church in Haiti be our prayer as well.

Lord,
We don't get mangos from
*   an avocado tree*
and we don't get corn
*   from a banana plant.*
We produce what we are.

> *Help us to be*
>   *What You need produced.*[37]

READING COLOSSIANS 1:24-2:7

Read this passage in a version of the Bible such as the NRSV, NIV, or NASB. And then read it in a paraphrase such as the Living Bible or the Message. Then read the passage a third time in your version.

LESSON

THE CALLING

Paul spends much more time on his testimony in this passage, but his labors for the gospel of Jesus Christ and all he has endured would not be possible without his calling. In 1:25 Paul writes, "I became its servant according to God's commission that was given to me for you, to make the word of God fully known."

It is important to remember that Paul does not know the Christians at Colossae personally, so his reflections on his calling and his work serve as an introduction to them. Some have suggested that Paul is attempting to establish his authority with the Colossians in this passage, but I think David Garland is much closer to the truth that Paul's authority is already a given, and here he is simply explaining in more detail what it means for him to be a servant of the gospel.[38]

The Greek word that the NRSV translates as servant is *diakonos*, where we get our English word "deacon." A deacon is one who carries out the command of someone else. Some Bibles, including the Revised Standard Version, translate *diakonos* as "minister." And while that is a perfectly acceptable rendering here, the idea of a minister as a servant has been lost in contemporary culture. Thus,

---

37   S. Burdick, ed. *God Is No Stranger* (Grand Rapids: Baptist Haiti Mission, 1970), np.

38   David E. Garland, *Colossians/Philemon* (Grand Rapids: Zondervan, 1998), pp. 116-117.

the word servant better captures Paul's self-designation. This is important to emphasize as Paul calls himself a humble *diakonos*, a table servant. This is not a title for a dignitary or someone of high rank. Here Paul is reflecting the attitude of Jesus who also referred to himself as one who came to serve (Mark 10:34). The character of God's call on the Apostle Paul and on every believer is one of service to Jesus Christ and to others.

The Testimony

The validity of Paul's calling is found in his testimony, which is his work on behalf of the Colossians and also the church at Laodicea which was located some ten miles by road up the Lycus River. Paul wants the Colossians to know that his striving or struggling are also for the sake of believers he has never met personally. His calling is one of service to the church, and such service has led to suffering for Paul, but he accepts and embraces such difficulties because it is for the sake of the church and its mission including the Colossians, even though the Apostle has not established the church there. Paul does not specify how the Colossians benefit from Paul's mission, but he could possibly have in mind his almost singular focus on bringing the gospel to the Gentiles, which has opened the door the others to engage in such mission.

Paul writes that his suffering completes "what is lacking in Christ's afflictions" (1:24). The Apostle is not suggesting that somehow his sufferings are a redemptive addendum to the suffering of Christ on the cross,[39] but rather that Paul is experiencing, as all believers experience, the suffering that often is necessary in the spread of the gospel. As David Garland eloquently observes, "Suffering comes with the territory of serving the gospel."[40] It could well be that Paul is adapting a particular Jewish view of tribulation

---

39   See Douglas J. Moo, *The Letters to the Colossians and to Philemon* (Grand Rapids: Eerdmans, 2008), pp. 152-153.

40   David E. Garland, *Colossians/Philemon*, (Grand Rapids: Zondervan, 1998), p. 120.

as a necessary element as a precursor to the new age.[41] What exactly Paul and Timothy believed about the return of Christ is difficult to say. Some have argued that the Apostle believed Christ would return during his lifetime, but modified his view as he grew older and approached death. Such a view cannot be ruled out, but it could also be the case that Paul expected the return of the Lord at any time—in his life or after his death. Thus, he could speak about the imminent return of Jesus while also speaking of his readiness for death (Philippians 1:21-24).

Paul interprets his sufferings as providing valid testimony to his calling as an Apostle. He wants the Colossians and the church at Laodicea (2:1) to be aware of his trials so that they too will be encouraged in the midst of their trials and that as a community of faith they will "be encouraged and united in love" (2:2). Difficult times often remind people of what is most important in life.

THE MYSTERY REVEALED

What is the mystery that Paul and Timothy speak of in Colossians? In Judaism a divine mystery could only be revealed by God himself. It could not be discovered by human beings as if God had hidden it somewhere and only the insightful could discern it. Only divine revelation can unwrap the mystery of which Paul speaks. In plain terms, the mystery now revealed in Christ is that from the beginning God intended to offer salvation to the Gentiles as equally as to Jews. The covenant and promises made to Israel was for the ultimate purpose of offering the new covenant and God's promises to the world. The plan of salvation comes through Israel, but it is not offered solely to Israel. Some accused Paul of taking the ancestral faith off on a destructive detour. Paul's claim is that in Jesus Christ, God is bringing the ancestral faith to its fulfillment. The promises to Israel are not revoked; they are now offered to all. Everyone gets to share in the inheritance by faith. Gentiles do

---

41 James D.G. Dunn, *The Epistles to the Colossians and Philemon* (Grand Rapids: Eerdmans, 1996), pp. 114-115.

not have to become Jews to be Christians. Again, I refer to David Garland,

> The mystery revealed to Paul was that God intended to save the Gentiles *from the very beginning*. Christ "among the Gentiles" was not Plan B after the gospel had been rejected by Jews. Rather, it was God's eternal purpose. The letter to Ephesians develops this idea more fully: "His purpose was to create in himself one new man out of the two, thus making peace, and in this one body to reconcile both of them to God through the cross, by which he put to death their hostility" (Eph, 2:15b-16). Christ "among the Gentiles" and "the hope of glory" for them was startling news to many Jews. For Gentiles it was the good news that should cause them to rejoice. Paul rejoices because God has chosen him to make this mystery known to Gentiles everywhere. Even though it has cost him an enormous toll in suffering, Paul rejoices to be an active participant in God's astounding plan for creation.[42]

The mystery now revealed in Jesus Christ fulfills the vision and hope of Abraham and Sarah that their descendants would number the stars in the night sky and the grains of sand on the seashore (Genesis 15:1-6; 22:17). It is only in Christ that these treasures of wisdom and knowledge are found.

THE NEED FOR GROWTH

The trials and tribulations of Paul did not discourage him and cause him to give up on his mission. Indeed, his suffering reminded him of the all-important nature of his call. In writing to the Colossians, Paul appeals to his own example as encouragement for the Colossians to continue to walk in the way of Christ even though the local synagogue is insisting that they are not living in the way of the ancestral Jewish faith in their unwillingness to take of the badges of ethnic identity that marked out first-century Jews as God's people. Paul knows how many Christians in Galatia

---

42   David E. Garland, *Colossians/Philemon*, (Grand Rapids: Zondervan, 1998), p. 126..

had succumbed to the temptation to take up such practices many years before (Galatians 4:8-11). The Colossians have not yet been persuaded, and Paul means to keep it that way. Thus the Colossians must continue to live their lives in Christ "rooted and built up in him and established in the faith" (2:6-7). To resort to Torah observance is tantamount to the Colossians returning to their former pagan ways.

DISCUSSION QUESTIONS

1. When have you believed God calling you to do something? What was it and how was that call confirmed?
2. It is clear from Colossians that testimony is important to Paul. How can testimony lead someone to Christian faith or lead a Christian into a deeper relationship with Jesus? When can testimony undermine the witness to the gospel?
3. Paul and Timothy write that in Christ the great mystery of Gentile salvation has now been revealed, but not all mysteries are made known. There are still plenty of things we do not know about the ways of God in this world. When you finally get to meet Jesus in eternity what one question would you ask him?
4. Paul tells the Colossians that they must continue to be "rooted and built up" in Christ and "established in the faith." What is necessary for us to heed Paul's words? How does the church assist individual believers in such progress toward spiritual maturity?

EXERCISE

As you read through Colossians 1:24-2:7, write down questions you would like to ask for further discussion.

On a piece of paper make three columns. In the first column list the practices necessary for spiritual growth as a Christian. In the second column write down how you are attending to each practice. In the last column take note of what you need to do to attend more faithfully to those practices.

HISTORICAL/THEOLOGICAL REFLECTION

The founder of Methodism, John Wesley (1703-1791) deeply believed in the spiritual disciplines and practices necessary for a vital relationship with Jesus Christ. Such practices included what he called "constant Communion," prayer and fasting, the reading of Scripture and works of charity. Wesley was very clear that there could be no division between inward piety and outward acts of charity.

CLOSING PRAYER

Ignatius of Loyola (1491-1556), the founder of the Jesuits (Society of Jesus) was deeply committed to Christ and the church. He made a vow to live in poverty, chastity, and obedience. In the Catholic Church Ignatius is the patron saint of spiritual retreats. He is the author of the following prayer:

> *Teach us, Good Lord, To Serve you as you deserve; To give and not to count the cost; To fight and not to heed the wounds; To toil and not to seek for rest; To labor and not to ask for any reward, save that of knowing that we do your will. Through Jesus Christ Our Lord, Amen.*

LESSON 5
LIVING LIFE IN CHRIST'S FULLNESS
(COLOSSIANS 2:8-23)

OBJECTIVE

The objective of this lesson is to reflect upon Jesus Christ as the focus of the new life and the lens through which all of life is to be viewed. Participants will be challenged to think about their own lives and ask where they have succumbed to the temptation to make non-essentials into necessary articles of faith. They will also be asked to reflect upon how one determines what beliefs and practices are indispensable to Christianity and what doctrines and habits are on the periphery.

OPENING PRAYER

Let us pray that God will help us in this lesson to focus on the important matters of our faith.

> *Gracious God, life is filled with so many distractions that it is difficult to keep the essential things of our faith at the center. We get so focused on the trivial that Jesus said will "rot away" (Matthew 6:19-20), we forget the weightier matters of justice, mercy, and faith (Matthew 23:23). In the midst of the noise and clutter of the daily routine help us to keep our attention on you knowing that even in the little matters we are to reflect the divine image in us, Jesus Christ, who with you and the Holy Spirit are one God now and forever Amen.*

READING COLOSSIANS 2:8-23

Read through Colossians 2:8-23 in three different versions. After that, read the passage in *The Message*.

LESSON

In 2:18-23, Paul and Timothy get to the heart of their argument. The Gentile Christians in the Colossian church are being told that their faith in Christ is insufficient, and that to be the true people of God they have to take upon themselves the observance of Torah. (Review my section above, "Why Was the Letter Written?") The writers of the letter will now argue otherwise.

CHRIST IS SUFFICIENT

It is important to state at the beginning that the Jewish practices that Paul highlights are beliefs and practices that by the first century A.D. had become identity markers for the Jewish people, specifically circumcision, the observing of certain food laws, and Sabbath observance (more detail on this below). Perhaps an illustration will help. If you were to travel back to first century Rome where there was a substantial Jewish population, and able to ask any Roman what a Jew was, they would likely respond in the following way: "A Jew is someone who will only worship one god. Some Romans wonder if they are atheists since they will not make an image of that god. Jews also circumcise all their male babies, they prepare their food in strange ways and there are certain foods they are prohibited from eating. They take one day a week, which they call the Sabbath, and they will do no work. They worship their imageless god and rest."

By Paul's day these practices had become boundary markers for Jews as the people of God. They were badges of identity. The synagogue in Colossae is criticizing the church for claiming to share in Israel's inheritance in Jesus Christ without taking up the outward practices that marked God's people off from everyone else. Paul and Timothy use terminology and references to specific practices that help us identify the specific nature of the criticism. These identity-forming practices for Judaism are all referred to in Colossians. More detail on these practices is necessary.

Circumcision—In Paul's day, circumcision had become one of the most important visible marks of the people of God, the nation of Israel. It was fundamental to Jewish identity.[43] Jewish scholars have simply assumed this to be the case.[44] It is interesting that Paul connects circumcision to baptism in Colossians 2:12-13. This is the only place in all of the letters of Paul where this connection is explicitly made. Perhaps the authors are making this connection as a contrast. Circumcision, the initiation rite for Israel, the people of God is now paralleled in baptism, the rite of initiation for the people of God the church. The "circumcision without hands" in 2:11 is set as the antithesis of physical circumcision, and it is a circumcision done in Christ. It seems likely that when Paul mentions the "circumcision of Christ" he is referring to Jesus' crucifixion. As circumcision is a cutting off of flesh, so Christ's death is a cutting off from humanity in order to offer salvation to that same humanity. In Christ's death God nails to the cross the handwritten document (v. 14), which is probably a reference to the Law of Moses. In so doing God has done away with circumcision as a requirement for God's people. The spiritual circumcision of the Colossians, the initiation into the covenant, took place for the Christians "through faith" (2:12).

Circumcision was a mark of the Jew and the covenant people. It bore witness to one's nationality. As a Jew, Paul had believed in the solidarity of the racial people of God. Colossians in no way rejects the solidarity of the people of God. What is rejected is solidarity defined in racial terms. The people of God are a people, but they are no longer marked by a rite tied inextricably to one

---

43   James D. G. Dunn, *Jesus Paul and the Law: Studies in Mark and Galatians* (Louisville: WJKP, 1990), p. 217.

44   Shaye J.D. Cohen, "Crossing the Boundary and Becoming a Jew," *The Harvard Theological Review* Vol. 82, No 1 (January 1989), pp. 13-33.

racial group. Paul and Timothy suggest that those who have receive this "circumcision without hands" need no other. The Jewish rite of circumcision is unnecessary and unimportant for faith in Christ and the membership of the people of God.

It could be said, therefore, that like circumcision for the Jew, baptism for the Christian is a mark or badge of identity, but unlike circumcision in Judaism baptism is not a badge that identifies with an ethnic people. Baptism does not signify that one is a Jew or a Gentile, but that one is a Christian.

Thus Christ is sufficient because his work on the cross is sufficient. There is nothing else that is necessary. If indeed the Colossians find circumcision to be necessary, that clearly means that Jesus' atoning death is not enough. But Paul is very clear. The Colossians have come to fullness in Christ who is "the head over every ruler and authority" (2:10). In this phrase the writers harken to the Christ-hymn of 1:15-20. If indeed, Jesus is the very wisdom of God, an affirmation previously given to the Law of Moses, the Torah, then Jesus himself has the authority even over the Law of Moses. Circumcision is no longer necessary because the very wisdom of God incarnate who gave the Torah has the authority to render its practice no longer necessary. In the Sermon on the Mount (Matthew 5-7) Jesus takes such authority over the Law.

The authors remind the Colossians in 2:13 of their way of life as Gentiles before coming to faith in Jesus Christ. Now that they are in Christ this lifestyle has been abandoned, even though the Colossians remain as Gentiles Their uncircumcision was made circumcision not with a rite done by human hands but by God who made them alive together with Christ forgiving their trespasses. Previously they were Gentiles outside the covenant, but now they are Gentiles inside the covenant, or at least, they are now Gentiles who participate in the promise (see Galatians 4:28). The promise is no longer for Jews and Gentiles who proselytize and take up the yoke of the law including the rite of circumcision. The promise is now made available to Jews as Jews and Gentiles as Gentiles.

Sabbath and Special Days—By the time of Jesus and Paul, Sabbath and special days and feasts had become marks of distinction associated with the people of God Israel and a critical sign of a Jew's faithfulness as a member of Israel.[45] In 1 Maccabees we read:

> The king then issued a decree throughout his empire: his subjects were all to become one people and abandon their own laws and religion. The nations everywhere complied with the royal commandment, and many in Israel accepted the foreign worship, sacrificing to idols and profaning the Sabbath (1 Maccabees. 1:41-43; cf. Isaiah 56:6; *Jubilees* 2:17-33; 50:6-13; Josephus *Antiquities,* 11:346).

In Jubilees the seasons and festivals are ordained as "feast for a memorial forever" (6:23-29; cf. 6:17-22, 35; 16:28-29; 49). The evidence indicates that the Sabbath was an observance unique to the people of Israel and by the first century CE it was a distinctively Jewish practice.[46]

In Colossians 2:16, Paul and Timothy refer to "festivals, new moons, and Sabbaths." This is a typical list of holy days found in the Old Testament.

> But this shall be the obligation of the prince regarding the burnt offerings, at the festivals, the new moons, and the Sabbaths, all the appointed festivals of the house of Israel (Ezekiel 45:17). I will put an end to all her mirth, her festivals, her new moons, her Sabbaths, and all her appointed festivals (Hosea 2:11).

Along with the mention of circumcision, it certainly appears that Jewish holy days are in mind. Moreover, since Sabbath is clearly a Jewish holy day, it's association with festivals and new moons indicate they too are Jewish in character (cf. 1 Chronicles

---

45 N. T. Wright, *The New Testament and the People of God*, (London: SPCK, 1992), p. 233.

46 James D.G. Dunn, *The Partings of the Ways: Between Christianity and Judaism and their Significance for the Character of Christianity* (London: SCM Press, 1991), pp. 29-30.

23:31; 2 Chronicles 2:3-5; 31:3; Nehemiah 10:33; Isaiah 1:13-14; Ezekiel 45:17; Hosea 2:11; 1 Maccabees 10:34). The use of the plural "Sabbaths" here is commonly Jewish.[47]

Food Laws—Food laws prescribed in the law of Moses were also a clear mark of Jewish identity in the first century world. Leviticus and Deuteronomy contain admonitions concerning unclean foods in and of themselves as well as foods offered to idols (Leviticus 3:17; 7:26-27; 11; 17:10-14; Deuteronomy 12:16, 23-24; 14; 15:23).[48] In the book of Daniel, we read that in exile Daniel refuses to contaminate himself with a diet in violation of the Torah.

> The king assigned a daily allowance of food and wine from the royal table... Now Daniel determined not to contaminate himself by touching the food and wine assigned to him by the king, and he begged the master of the eunuchs not to make him do so (Daniel 1:5, 8; cf. 10:3).

It is important to note that the Jewish diet was known as a distinctive mark of Jewishness to Gentile.[49]

The two phrases found in Colossians in reference to Jewish dietary laws are found in 2:16, "matters of food and drink," and 2:21, "'Do not handle,' 'Do not taste,' 'Do not touch.'" While it is the case that Jews weren't the only people to observe dietary regulations of some sort, it seems that along with circumcision, and festival and Sabbath observance, Jewish kosher regulations are in mind. Diaspora Jews were particularly concerned over whether both food and drink had previously been offered to the pagan gods. Colossians 2:21, where the authors are possibly quoting the Colossian philosophers, "Do not handle. Do not taste. Do not touch," an Old Testament flavor can be detected. There is a

---

47 Lightfoot, *Colossians*, p. 192.

48 See James D.G. Dunn, *The Partings of the Ways: Between Christianity and Judaism and their Significance for the Character of Christianity* (London: SCM Press, 1991), p. 130.

49 See Allan R. Bevere, *Sharing in the Inheritance: Identity and the Moral Life in Colossians* (Sheffield: Sheffield Academic Press, 2003), pp. 79-90.

particularly striking passage in the (first century CE) Testament of Moses:

> They, with hand and mind, will touch impure things, yet their mouths will speak enormous things, and they will even say, "do not touch me, lest you pollute me in the position I occupy..." (7:9-10).

Colossians 2:21 also reflects rabbinic teaching:

> If a Nazarite drank wine throughout the day, he is liable (for scourging) only on one count. If they said to him (as often as he proposes to drink), "Do not drink! Do not drink!" and he drank (nevertheless), he is liable on each count. If he contracted uncleanness because of the dead throughout the day, he is liable (for scourging) on only one count. If they say to him, "Do not contract uncleanness! Do not contract uncleanness!" and he (nevertheless) contracted uncleanness, he is liable on each count (Talmud, *Makkoth* 3.7).

It is clear that such dietary concerns were an important feature of life in the Jewish world of Paul. Moreover, the reference to all of these practices as "a shadow of what is to come" (2:17) is reminiscent of Hebrews 10:1— "Since the law has only a shadow of the good things to come and not the true form of these realities, it can never, by the same sacrifices that are continually offered year after year, make perfect those who approach." These badges of Jewish ethnic identity, that marked out Israel as God's people were a shadow, a foreshadowing of what was to come. Nowhere in his letters does Paul ever suggest that Christianity has made Judaism irrelevant; rather Christianity is the fulfillment of Judaism, which represented the shadow of what God now intends in Jesus Christ.[50] If the Colossians were to listen to the warnings of the Colossian philosophers and resort to such Torah observance, it would be tantamount to returning to their pagan way of which Paul reminds

---

50 N.T. Wright, *Colossians and Philemon*, Tyndale New Testament Commentaries (Downers Give: IVP Academic, 2008), p. 119.

them in 2:13. Such ways are now in Christ nothing more than "human commands and teachings" (2:22), and not the divine way now prepared for them in Christ Jesus.

Jesus is indeed sufficient for the Christians in Colossae. Nothing else is necessary.

DISCUSSION QUESTIONS

1. Paul and Timothy remind the Christians at Colossae to keep the main thing the main thing. They do not want the Colossians to get distracted with the non-essentials. The temptation for Christians and the church in general is to major in the minors and forget what is at the center of our faith and life. On what non-essentials have Christians and entire churches focused on that has distracted them away from their calling and purpose? In what ways have we sent the message that Jesus is not sufficient?

2. Part of the problem Paul sees with the emphasis of the Colossian philosophers on these outward practices of the law is that they exclude the Gentile Christians from full participation in the community of faith, and that they do not share equally with Jews in the inheritance of salvation. Where has the church intentionally and unintentionally insisted on things that exclude others?

3. What are the boundary markers, the badges of identity that reveal you and your church to be Christians? There's a popular campfire chorus that goes, "They will know we are Christians by our love." Is love all we need or are others things necessary for people to know we are followers of Jesus?

EXERCISE

Read through Colossians 2:8-23 again. Write down words or phrases that you would like to understand more fully. Consult a commentary or two for assistance.

Share a time when you felt excluded from the church community. What was the particular reason? Think also of a time when you may have unintentionally excluded someone else? How did that take place?

HISTORICAL/THEOLOGICAL REFLECTION

While baptism can signify cleansing and forgiveness of sin, it is also the rite of initiation into the covenant community called the church, as is inferred in Colossians 2:14. When I baptize children or adults, the congregation offers the following response of love and support to the baptized:

> With God's help we will proclaim the good news and live according to the example of Christ. We will surround these persons with a community of love and forgiveness, that they may grow in their trust of God, and be found faithful in their service to others. We will pray for them, that they may be true disciples who walk in the way that leads to life.[51]

Just before I ask the congregation to make this pledge, I say to them, "Remember your baptism and be thankful. When I utter these words, I am not asking them to literally remember the day they were baptized, since many of them were baptized as infants and have no memory of that day. What I am asking them to do in that moment is to remember that they, like the persons just baptized, are members of this covenant community we call the church and that we have a mutual obligation to care for one another and a common mission to make disciples of Jesus Christ. They are being asked to remember who they are "in Christ" (Colossians 1:2). William Willimon writes,

> To the pressing "Who am I?" question, the church has traditionally responded, "You are baptized."
> .... In baptism, God acts through the church, in water, to enlarge the family of God and to save them by joining them to the death and resurrection of Christ. In baptism we are initiated, crowned, chosen, embraced, washed, adopted, gifted, reborn, killed, and thereby sent forth and redeemed. We are

---

51   *The United Methodist Hymnal* (1989), p. 35.

identified as one of God's own, then assigned our place and our job within the kingdom of God

The way for a Christian to find out who he or she is, is not to jump on the rear of a Honda and head west, but rather to come to the font and look into those graceful waters. The reflection of yourself which you see there is who you really are.[52]

CLOSING PRAYER

We thank you, God, for the gift of creation made known to us in water and word. Before the world had shape and form, your Spirit moved over the waters. Out of the waters of the deep, you formed the firmament and brought forth the earth to sustain all life. In the time of Moses, your people Israel passed through the Red Sea waters from slavery to freedom and crossed the flowing Jordan to enter the promised land. You have come to us through water in the stories of Jesus who was nurtured in the water of Mary's womb, baptized by John in the water of the Jordan, and became living water to a woman at the Samaritan well. Jesus washed the feet of the disciples and sent them forth to baptize with water and spirit. Bless by your Holy Spirit, gracious God, this water. Bless all who touch and taste this water that may be ever reminded of your abiding presence and claim on their lives. Amen.[53]

---

52   William H. Willimon, *Remember Who You Are: Baptism, a Model for Christian Life* (Nashville: The Upper Room, 1980), p. 108.
53   "Liturgy for Infant Baptism," http://liturgyoutside.net/ BaptismalLiturgy.html.

LESSON 6
LIVING THE HEAVENLY LIFE ON EARTH
(COLOSSIANS 3:1-17)

OBJECTIVE

Eternal life happens now. It is not something to be achieved after we die. We participate in the new life in the present. St. Paul writes, "Since you have been raised with Christ." What it means to participate in Jesus' resurrection now makes a difference for how we live now. As people of the resurrection, Christians are to offer in word and in deed that new life of Jesus in the present. We must reflect on the forms that such new life may take in the here and now.

OPENING PRAYER

READING COLOSSIANS 3:1-17

The fact that Colossians participate in Christ is crucial to Paul's ethical admonitions to come. It is true that all of the various themes of Paul's ethics in Colossians are inevitably connected to Christ. What Barclay says of Galatians is also true of Colossians— "Thus

---

54 *The Revised Common Lectionary,* http://lectionary.library. vanderbilt.edu/prayers.php?id=85.

in one sense it could be said that all of Paul's ethics derive from 'participation in Christ'."[55]

Paul begins Chapter 3, "Since *you have been* raised with Christ." In other words, Paul is saying that since you now live in Jesus' resurrection, live as if that is indeed the case. Live in the truth of the resurrection. Heaven and earth are not two separate entities. As Jesus teaches his disciples in the Lord's Prayer, "thy kingdom come, they will be done on earth as it is in heaven." The resurrection life of Jesus is available now for those who believe.

The Christians in Colossae are encouraged to look heavenward, not to escape this world, but rather to put this world in heavenly context, to seek the things above is not an escape from earthly realities, but rather the things above put earthly things in their divine context.

The resurrection of Jesus in history brings heaven to earth. In these opening verses in Colossians Chapter 3, Paul and Timothy remind their readers that heaven and earth are intermingled together.

The fact that the Colossians participate in Christ is crucial to Paul's ethical admonitions. It is true that all the various themes of Paul's ethics in Colossians are inevitably connected to Christ.

Paul and Timothy tell the believers in Colossae to put to death the vices within them and put on the clothing of the resurrected life. Right from the beginning of Colossians, Paul wants to remind the Colossians that their whole Christian existence is bound up with Jesus Christ. To participate in the new life in Christ is to be directed onward toward the "things above." The emphasis in Colossians on wisdom and understanding of God is the key that unlocks wisdom itself.[56] The Colossian Christians have been tempted to look for God's wisdom elsewhere. Paul and Timothy are clear that the Colossians have access to divine wisdom through Jesus Christ.

---

55 John M.G. Barclay, *Obeying the Truth: Paul's Ethic in Galatians* (Minneapolis: Fortress Press, 1988), p. 224.

56 N.T. Wright, *Colossians and Philemon,* Tyndale New Testament Commentaries (Downers Give: IVP Academic, 2008), p. 95.

It is true that there is still a hiddenness to their lives in Christ, yet to be revealed (3:4). This is part of that mystery of which Paul speaks in 2:3. Yet the revelation of Jesus Christ in the lives of the Colossians is a process already begun as well. The mystery revealed is that the Gentile believers are reconciled to Christ, and are being formed after Christ's image to be holy and blameless. The only requirement given to the Colossians to continue on this journey is that they continue securely established in the faith, without shifting from the hope promised (1:23).

Paul makes an interesting point in 3:3. He says, "when Christ who is our life." Paul does not seem to believe that Christ will be our lives only in the future, but that Christ is our life in the present. The Colossian Christians stand in the resurrection life of Jesus. This means that a way of life has been prescribed for them while certain vices must be rejected.

Christian Ethical Living—"Christian ethics depends upon the resurrection of Jesus Christ from the dead."[57] The resurrection of Jesus makes the believer strong, able to endure all things patiently (1:11). The Colossians through faith have been transferred into the kingdom of his beloved Son (1:13), in whom the Colossians find forgiveness that is only possible because of his resurrection (2:13). The cross of Christ and his resurrection are kept close together at all times throughout the letter; especially in 2:11-15 when mention is made of the Colossians' burial with Christ in baptism, and their resurrection with him through faith.

The foundation of the moral instruction in Colossians is the community's participation in the cross and resurrection of Christ. Paul and Timothy continually remind their readers of this throughout the letter. In 2:20 we read, "If with Christ you died to the elemental spirits of the universe, why do you live as if you still belonged to the world?" The Colossians are admonished "to put to death" all that is "of the earth" (3:5) as they have stripped off "the old

---

57 Oliver O'Donovan, *Resurrection and Moral Order: An Outline of Evangelical Ethics* (Leicester: InterVarsity Press, 1986), p. 13.

self with its practices" (3:9). It is interesting to note that since the first ethical reference to the resurrection of Christ comes in 3:1— "Since therefore you have been raised with Christ," Paul will then describe how that resurrection life is to look in the church—God's Easter people. Paul uses the language of clothing. The Christians at Colossae must put on the new self with its practices listed in 3:12-17). But before they can put on their Christian moral clothing, they must first take of the clothing of their former way of life. Paul and Timothy will address that first.

Vices, the Clothing of the Old Self—Since our authors have highlighted the cross of Christ and its importance, it is not a surprise that Paul and Timothy refer to the Colossians' old selves as something to be killed, as something that must be put to death (3:5). This former earthly way of life, which the letter has previously referred to as "estranged and hostile in mind, doing evil deeds" (1:21) is contrary to the resurrected life the Colossians now enjoy. One cannot pretend to live in light of Jesus' death and resurrection while living as if they never happened.

Paul goes into specific detail as to the character of that earthly life by listing a series of vices, behaviors that are unacceptable for God's Easter people. We will take each one in turn.

Fornication—The Greek word translated "fornication" is *porneia*, from whence we get the English word "pornography." *Porneia* can refer specifically to Prostitution, and generally to all sorts of extra-marital sexual behavior.[58] Cult prostitution in the Greek and Roman worlds in Asia Minor (modern day Turkey) was common.[59] Prostitution in general was accepted because sexual intercourse was understood as natural as eating and drinking. The exception to this in Paul's day was Judaism, which reserved sexual intercourse only for the covenant of marriage. In Jewish writings

---

58   Reisser, "πορνεύω," *The New International Dictionary of New Testament Theology*, Vol. 1 (Regency Reference Library, 1986), p. 497.

59   James D. G. Dunn, *The Theology of Paul's Letter to the Galatians* (Cambridge: Cambridge University Press, 1993), p. 303.

porneia was also used to refer to such practices as incest. In the Greek world it was often considered permissible for a married man to have extra-marital sex as long as his civil marriage was not violated. Yet such behavior was often forbidden for the wife.[60] In Judaism extra-marital sex was forbidden for both men and women.

Impurity—the next word, *akatharsia*, which is often translated "impurity," elaborates on the first word, *porneia*. *Akatharsia* can refer to religious and moral impurity (e.g. Plato, *Laws* 4.716e). The LXX links the Hebrew word to ritual purity (Genesis 7:2; Leviticus 4:12). Since moral purity is important in Israel's worship of God, such purity inevitably is connected to ritual purity (practices of worship). The worship of God and immoral purity are mutually exclusive of one another (Isaiah 52:11; cf. Romans 1:24-25; 2 Corinthians 12:21; Galatians 5:19; Ephesians 5:3; Revelation 17:4).

While religious and moral purity are often directed at the Israelites, a definite connection is made in Judaism between impurity and Gentile idolatry,[61] particularly when the term is used with *porneia*. It is clear when reading Paul's letters, *akatharsia* is used to refer to sexual impurity with definite pagan connotations (Romans 1:24; 6:19; 2 Corinthians 12:21; Ephesians 4:19; 5:3; 1 Thessalonians 4:7). For the Jew of the first century, it was a proud thing to contrast his purity with the impurity of the Gentiles.[62] Here in Colossians Paul and Timothy use *akatharsia* to refer to "the immoral state of the pre-Christian life."[63]

Passion—In Stoic philosophy persons who let themselves be controlled by their emotions can be described by the word

---

60   See Hauck and Schulz, "πόρνεια κτλ," *Theological Dictionary of the New Testament,* Vol. VI (Grand Rapids: Eerdmans, 1969), p. 583.

61   Petr Pokorný, *Colossians: A Commentary* (Peabody: Hendrickson, 1987), p. 166.

62   Eduard Lohse, *Colossians and Philemon* (Philadelphia: Fortress Press, 1971), p. 138, n. 12.

63   Hauck, "ακαθαρσία," Theological Dictionary of the New Testament, III, pp. 428-429.

"passion," which in Greek is *pathos*. Here in Colossians it refers to "shameful passion that leads to sexual excesses."[64] (See also Galatians 5:24). This is a very Jewish use of the term. This is especially true when *pathos* is combined with the next word, *epithumia*, which the NRSV translates, "evil desire."

Evil Desire—While the word *epithumia* was not always employed in negative fashion (Jesus uses the term in Luke 22:15 to refer to his desire to eat the Passover with the disciples.), it's use in this context makes it clear that Paul is using the term negatively. Not all desires are evil, but Paul specifically has evil desires in mind in Colossians. In Numbers 11 and Genesis 39 in the LXX *epithumia* is the longing for sexual satisfaction outside of marriage and is referred to as sin.[65] In Matthew, Mark, and Luke (called the synoptic gospels) and in Paul's letters the word often refers to sexual desire (Matthew 5:28; Romans 1:24; 1 Thessalonians 4:15).[66] In Judaism such desire is prohibited. It is an offense against God who demands complete devotion from his people.

Greed (which is idolatry)—The last two vices listed in 3:5 are connected together.

Pleoneksía (greed) and *eidōlolatria* (idolatry). In Jewish thinking "[t]he two sins stood together... and were condemned as part of the horrors of paganism."[67]

In non-Jewish, non-Christian usage idolatry did not customarily refer to images of gods, but in the LXX, the word is used to translate Hebrew words that refer exclusively to pagan deities and the images used to portray them (e.g. 1 Samuel 31:9; 1 Chronicles 10:9; 2 Chronicles 24:18; Psalms 115:4; 135:15 Isaiah 10:11; 48:5; Hosea 4:17; 8:4; 13:2; 14:9; Micah 1:7; Zechariah

---

64   Eduard Lohse, *Colossians and Philemon* (Philadelphia: Fortress Press, 1971), p. 138.

65   Büchsel, "θυμός," *Theological Dictionary of the New Testament*, Vol. III (Grand Rapids: Eerdmans, 1966), p. 169.

66   Pokorný, *Colossians: A Commentary* (Peabody: Hendrickson, 1987), p. 166.

67   Peter T. O'Brien, *Colossians, Philemon* (Waco: Word, 1982), p. 177.

13:2). Such portrayals are always negative. Thus the usage of the various Greek forms of *eidōlolatria* in this way is uniquely Jewish.

The New Testament picks up this negative usage. The worship of pagan gods is categorically condemned (1 Corinthians 5:10-11; 6:9; 10:7, 14; 1 Peter 4:3). In Paul's letters Gentile Christians are consistently warned against idolatry not only because pagan temples and idols were everywhere, but also because many Gentile Christians thought it possible to combine the worship of several different deities while following Jesus.[68] It was therefore important to remind the Gentile believers at Colossae that by virtue of their faith in Christ, they inherited the strict monotheism of Judaism.

When idolatry and greed are combined together the focus is on humanity and not God. The distinction between creator and creature is blurred, and idolatry is the result (see Matthew 6:24). The greedy person lacks the knowledge of God (Romans 1:29; 1 Corinthians 5:10, 11; 6:10, 11; Ephesians 5:3). Indeed, greed can become idol worship because greedy persons are so focused on themselves and what they want, their life pursuits become a form of self-worship. They become their own idols.

Anger, Wrath, Malice—After a brief reminder to the Colossians that the way of these vices are formerly familiar to them but no longer, Paul and Timothy return to their list of vices in verses 8 and 9.

The first vice listed in verse 9 is translated as "anger" by the NRSV, but a more concise rendering is "vehement rage." Here Paul is not referring to justified anger at injustice, which Jesus himself displayed.[69] The Greek word *thumos* (from whence we get our English words, "thermometer" and "thermos") refers to a resentful and grudging hatred that views other individuals as less than human and not worthy of being treated as created in the image of God. This is especially true when used with the next vice listed,

---

68 N. T. Wright, *The New Testament and the People of God* (London: SPCK, 1992), p. 155.

69 See "What Makes Jesus Angry?" http://www.relevantmagazine.com/god/worldview/what-makes-jesus-angry.

"wrath." Such anger and wrath are signs of malice or wickedness, which speaks directly to the character of those who exhibit such vices.

In verses eight and nine, Paul and Timothy also list the practices the Colossians are to rid from their lives—slander and abusive language—demeaning one's reputation and uttering obscenities toward them. These practices are exhibited by those who have embodied the vices mentioned. Such practices tear at the fabric of unity the church is supposed to embody and display. Being raised with Christ means a new community with unity at its heart.

The New Humanity: Unity in Diversity—The admonitions of Paul to strip off the old way of life with its vices and evil practices are not optional for those who are in Christ. In the work of Christ God has brought into existence the church, a new and redeemed community unified by the power of the Holy Spirit and diverse in the gifts it offers in the fulfillment of that mission. A new humanity leads to a new way of life. Colossians 3:11 marks a transitional verse from the vices to the virtues. The vices already mentioned are a reminder as to what hinders unity; the virtues are the habits that bring unity. But this unity in Christ is not just about diverse people getting along and tolerating each other. This unity is radically new and unlike anything seen before. Paul describes that renovation in Christ in 3:11: "In that renewal there is no longer Greek or Jew, circumcised and uncircumcised, barbarian, Scythian, slave and free; but Christ is all and in all."

It is important to note that the Jew/Gentile distinction is mentioned twice. (The term "Greek" is used as a synonym for Gentile.) As I have suggested, the character of the Colossian philosophy was Jewish, so this double-emphasis is not a surprise. What is meant by the Jew/Greek distinction is repeated and explicated further by the next distinction, "circumcision and uncircumcision." In Christ, the boundaries drawn between Jew and Gentile given in the law of Moses, of which circumcision was the most important, are no longer valid (cf. Galatians 6:15).

While the emphasis in 3:11 may concern the Jew/Gentile distinction, Paul and Timothy continue. Here in 3:11 we have an affirmation that is socially significant. In addition to Jew/Greek, and circumcision/uncircumcision, the terms "Barbarian" and "Scythian" are also of social importance. The Greeks themselves often distinguished between two kinds of people: Greeks and barbarians, and Scythians were even lower on the social scale.[70] Thus the pair barbarian/Scythian is to be interpreted in mutually exclusive categories. In Christ, such ethnic and cultural distinctions make no difference in the economy of God's salvation in Jesus Christ.

This new humanity that is birthed from Christ's work is indeed a unity. Paul and Timothy do not have in mind some kind of natural equality, whatever that might mean, but rather they envisage people from diverse backgrounds and cultural stations gathered together by one common Lord Their allegiance to that Lord means something for the way these Christians live in relationship to each other, even though they continue to live in the roles determined by the world. Salvation defined in nationalistic, ethnic, cultural, or economic terms will do nothing but divide the church.

Virtues, the Clothing of the New Self—Paul now turns his attention to the way of life that displays the unity of the body. Paul has spent some time listing the dispositions that are not in keeping with those who participate in the resurrected life of Christ, and that divide the church. Now he turns his attention to the virtues, the dispositions that reflect the new life in Christ and the new humanity embodied in the church, the Body of Christ.

Compassion—The Greek *splanchnic oiktirmou* can be translated "heartfelt mercy." *Splanchna* refers mainly to the entrails of sacrificial animals and later the term was used to refer to the sacrificial meal itself where the viscera were eaten.[71] Although mercy was not part of pre-Christian Greek usage, from the fifth century B.C. onward

---

70   See Martin Hengel, *Jews, Greeks, and Barbarians* (London: SCM Press, 1980), pp. 215-216.
71   Aristophanes, *The Birds*, 984.

splanchna refers to the location of a person's natural passions—anger, desire, and love. That *splanchna* denotes mercy or compassion is found only in Jewish and Christian writings.[72]

In Judaism, *splanchna* also refers to entrails, but in Proverbs 12:10 the *splanchna* without *oiktirmos* also refers to compassion. The use of the word in this way is more common in ancient literature (2 Maccabees 9:5; 4 Maccabees 5:30; 10:8; 11:19; 15:23; Wis. 10:5).

In the LXX *oiktirmos* refers first and foremost to God who acts compassionately on behalf of Israel (Psalms 24:6; 50:1; 104:4; 144:9; cf. Nehemiah 9:19, 27, 28). Connected to God's mercy is the notion that living according to God's will means that God's people will also have such mercy (2 Chronicles 30:9; Psalms 106:46; 1 QS 4:3). The New Testament picks up the same idea of God's compassion in Christ (Romans 12:1; 2 Corinthians 1:3). The same is true of *splancha*, particularly in reference to Christ's acts of compassion Matthew 9:36; 14:14; Mark 1:41; 9:22; Luke 7:13; cf. Matthew 18:27; Luke 10:33; 15:20). Here in Colossians 3:13, Paul and Timothy charge the Colossians to clothe themselves with the compassion of Christ.

Kindness—The NRSV translates the word *chrēstotēta* as kindness, but perhaps goodness or generosity is better. The word was also used to refer to someone who is honest and decent.[73] In the LXX, this word is used in the sense of excellence in reference to things genuine (Jeremiah 24:2, 3, 5) and costly (Ezekiel 27:22; 28:13; Daniel. 2:32). It is also used to refer to God's goodness and the faithfulness God exhibits to his people (Psalms 25:7; 31:19; 65:11. Such faithfulness is displayed even in the midst of the sins of the people (Jeremiah 33:11; 24:2, 3, 5).[74] In the Dead Sea scrolls, the word is used of the believers who are to show the same kindness

---

72   See Eduard Schweizer, *Letter to the Colossians* (Minneapolis: Augsburg, 1982), p. 205.

73   Sophocles, *Oedipus Tyrannus* 609-610; Aristotle, *Poetics* 15, 1454a, 16-18.

74   See Peter T. O'Brien, *Colossians, Philemon* (Waco: Word, 1982), pp. 199-200.

and benevolence that they received from God (1 QS 2.24; 5.4, 25; 8.2) Philo and Josephus use *chrēstòs* as kindness, gentleness, and graciousness.[75] In Colossians, *chrēstotēta* is a direct outworking of love. As God has acted graciously in Jesus Christ toward sinners so Christians must act graciously toward others.

Humility—It is interesting that Paul and Timothy list humility (*tapeinophrosýnēn*) as a Christian virtue. The Greeks did not consider humility a virtue at all. Humility was a sign of weakness and was considered a vice (Homer, *Odyssey* 17.322-323; Plato, *Laws* 5.728e; 6.744c; 7.791d; Euripides, *Andromache* 164-165; Xenophon, *Cyropaedia* 5.1.5). The Jewish historian Josephus, in writing for the Romans always uses the word humility in negative fashion (*War* 4.319, 365, 494; 6.395; *Ant.* 5.115; 7.95; 10.11; 13.415), which is a radical departure from his own Jewish heritage likely because his Roman audience would have understood the terminology in this way. Rarely, in this wider Grecian context is the word used positively, and often refers less to humility and more to obedience, which leads to humility, particularly in reference to obeying the laws of the gods.

The New Testament background of *tapeinophrosýnēn* is to be found, not in a Roman context, but in a Jewish one. In Judaism, humility is not shameful, but something necessary in one's relationship to God. the word humility and its related terms are used approximately 270 times in the LXX. It is used negatively in the sense of oppress or afflict (e.g. Genesis 34:2; Deuteronomy 21:14; 2 Samuel 13:12-14; Ezekiel 22:10-11, but for the most part this word group refers to what God has done to bring down the proud and haughty and lift up the poor and lowly (e.g. 1 Samuel 1:11; 2:8; 7:13; 2 Samuel 22:5, 28; Psalms 22:5, 28; Psalms 10:17-18; 25:18; Amos 2:6-7; Zechariah 2:3; 3:12.

In reference to human beings, humility is used positively (Job 5:11; Proverbs 3:34; 11:2; 15:33, cf. Ecclesiastes 10:6; Sirach 7:11;

---

75   See Allan R. Bevere, *Sharing in the Inheritance: Identity and the Moral Life in Colossians* (Sheffield: Sheffield Academic Press, 2003), p. 205.

10:15-17; 11:12-13) as necessary in life's experiences. The community at Qumran referred to themselves as poor and lowly which express the proper attitude one should have before God. Indeed, in the Dead Sea scrolls humility is listed with other virtues—lovingkindness, truth, faithfulness, and patience. It must be nurtured by the community, and they must admonish one another in humility, among other things (1QS 2.24; 4.3; 5.3, 25). The same perspective can be seen in the noncanonical Testaments of the Twelve Patriarchs (*Testament of Benjamin.* 5:5; *Testament of Judah* 19:2; *Testament of Joseph.* 10:2; 18:3). The Jewish philosopher Philo also views humility as a virtue.

This is the background of the positive usage of humility in Colossians 3:12 and in the New Testament generally. In the Gospels, humility is clearly the way to exaltation (Matthew 11:29; Luke 14:11; cf. Mark 10:15. Paul also uses the term in Romans 12:16 as a necessary virtue of the Christian disciple who is to imitate the Lord they follow (see Philippians 2:1-11, particularly v. 3; Acts 8:35). Where Paul does use the term negatively, it is always polemical (2 Corinthians 10:1; and of course Colossians 2:18, 23). Paul and Timothy do not view humility as weakness, but rather as consideration of others and the surrender of one's privileges.[76]

Meekness—The Greek word *praütēs* which the NRSV translates as meekness denotes that which is gentle and pleasant (Plato, *Laws* 10.888a; Xenophon, *Symposium*, 1.10). *Praütēs* reflects high ideals and social virtue.

Praütēs is used nineteen times in the LXX and translates Hebrew words that mean poor, humble, and meek (Job 24:4; Psalms 25:9; 34:2; 37:14; 149:4; Isaiah 32:7; Zephaniah 2:3; 3:12; Zechariah 9:9). The lack of pride and wealth is seen as virtuous (Sirach 1:27; 4:8; 10:28; Josephus. *Aniquitiest.* 19.328; 5.166-168; 6:7-9; 7.117-118).

Meekness is a virtue to be displayed by Christians. It is one of the concrete expressions of Christian love (Galatians 5:23;

---

76   Ralph Martin, *Colossians and Philemon* (Grand Rapids: Eerdmans, 1973), p. 11.

Colossians 3:12-14; 1 Timothy 6:11; 1 Peter 3:4). In the New Testament there is a divine source for such humility. In Colossians it is one of the results of being elected by God (3:12), in Galatians it is found in the work of the Holy Spirit (5:23, and in Ephesians it is a sign of one's calling (4:2).

Patience—In the LXX *makrothymían* often marks an attribute of God who restrains himself when it comes to the judgment of his people (Exodus 34:6; Numbers 14:18; Psalms 86:15; 103:8; Joel 2:13; Nahum 1:3). Since God is patient with his people, they too must be patient with others (Proverbs 14:29; 16:32; 25:15). It is important to note that some read the Old Testament and come away with a view of an impatient God who is quick to judge, but that is the wrong way to view the entire Old Testament narrative. Alden Thompson says of the portrayal of God in the Old Testament that a "God of incredible patience is a much more accurate description."[77]

A Crescendo of Unity and Love and Peace—The purpose of the clothing of the new humanity, this life of Christian virtue is now specifically laid out by Paul and Timothy and crescendos in 3:14: "Above all, clothe yourselves with love, which binds everything together in perfect harmony." It is not the case that these virtues listed in Colossians were unknown outside of a Christian context, but there is something decisively Christian about the context in which these particular virtues thrive. The virtues the Colossians are to clothe themselves with find their meaning in the reorientation of their lives "in Christ," "in the Lord." The Christian community lives by reflecting in its life the gospel which it proclaims. The gospel is formulated in 3:13b: "The Lord has forgiven you.[78]

As love binds together all the good dispositions of character, so it binds the community in "perfect harmony." This love stands not as an abstract, sentimental notion. It is the love the Colossians have experienced by virtue of their participation in Christ, and

---

77 Alden Thompson, *Who's Afraid of the Old Testament God?* (Gonzalez: Energion, 2001), p. 30.

78 Pokorný, *Colossians: A Commentary* (Peabody: Hendrickson, 1987), p. 171.

which was exemplified in the life and death of Christ. It is the kind of love that can only be practiced in the church that has died to the old order and has been resurrected to participate in the new. Love is the bond of unity secured by Christ in the power of the Holy Spirit in which a new humanity is brought together made up of Jew and Gentile and slave and free.

Love is the supreme virtue of grace. as suggested in the phrase "above all things." Love then can be thought of as the outer garment the believers wear that hold the inner garments of virtue in place. [79] Love leads to peace; but it is not a peace in general, but the "peace of Christ," which only those who are "in Christ" can enjoy.

It is God's will that his people live in peace and harmony. This is not the kind of peace that can be found simply through dialogue and mutual understanding. It is in Christ that such peace is possible and finds concrete expression. Those distinctions and lifestyle that stand in the way of this peace have been abolished and can no longer be tolerated. It is Christ's love embodied in his life, death, and resurrection, and his teaching which gives expression to the kind of peace that is to reign in the midst of the congregation. The believers in Colossae, though they are Gentiles, participate in this unity which is God's new creation. Therefore, everything they do should be done, not according to the law of Moses, but "in the name of Christ Jesus" (cf. 1 Corinthians 5:4; 6:11; Philippians 2:10). As wisdom found a home in Israel, so the word of Christ should be at home in the church.[80]

The garments of Christian virtue worn well, lead to a church that is faithful and loving and at peace.

DISCUSSION QUESTIONS

1. When most people think of eternal life they probably imagine life after our human bodies have died. But Paul is very clear

---

79   C.F.D. Moule, *The Epistles of Paul the Apostle to the Colossians and to Philemon* (Cambridge: Cambridge University Press, 1957), p. 123.

80   Eduard Lohse, *Colossians and Philemon* (Philadelphia: Fortress Press, 1971), p. 152.

in the first part of chapter three that disciples of Jesus Christ share in his resurrection here and now in this life. In what ways does God's gift of eternity affect us now?

2. One of the vices listed in Colossians 3 is greed. The Bible has much to say about materialism and yet we hear very little about the dangers of wealth in sermons and in Bible studies. Why does it seem that in the church we tend to avoid this particular sin?

3. Sometimes in the preaching and teaching of the church living as a Christian is boiled down to an ethic of just being nice to others. Yet, we certainly cannot believe that Jesus died on the cross just so that we could be nice. Paul and Timothy see the resurrection of Jesus as transforming life into something radical. As we reflect upon the Christian virtues listed by Paul what makes the Christian life radically different, as something much more than just being nice?

4. The church as God's new humanity in 3:11 is held together in unity. Yet, we know that all too often the church finds itself deeply divided. What are the things that undermine the unity of the Body of Christ that Paul and Timothy believed was so essential?

EXERCISE

Read Colossians 3:1-17 twice and write down any questions you would like to ask for further discussion.

Recall a time when either you or a Christian you know sacrificed something important in order to say or do the right thing because of their Christian convictions. What sacrifice was made and what was the outcome of the decision to do what was right?

HISTORICAL/THEOLOGICAL REFLECTION

The bodily resurrection of Jesus stands at the heart of Christian faith. If the tomb is not empty than as St. Paul says to the Corinthians, "If Christ has not been raised, your faith is futile and you are still in your sins. Then those also who have died in Christ have perished. If for this life only we have hoped in Christ, we are of all people most to be pitied" (1 Corinthians 15:17-19). But it is important to remember that when we refer to Jesus as being resurrected, we are not saying that he was just resuscitated, that is, he was brought back in the same mortal body he had prior to his death. In John chapter eleven Jesus resuscitates Lazarus, meaning Lazarus would die again; but Jesus was resurrected—his body was transformed into something that transcended death and decay. In his resurrection, Jesus had the same body he had prior to his death, but it was renewed and transformed.

So, there are two things that are important to say about Jesus' resurrection and our resurrections at the end of history. First, the resurrected state will be different from our present experience. Just as Jesus' resurrected body had qualities different from his body prior to death, our life in the new heavens and the new earth will be free from the limitations brought about by the fall of humanity and sin. We will be changed; flesh and blood cannot inherit the kingdom of God (1 Corinthians 15:50f.) Taking Jesus' resurrected body as our model, we meet new and strange properties (cf. Luke 24:13; 36ff.; John 20:19-29).

Second, our resurrected state will retain some continuity with our present experience, just as we see with Jesus. Who we are now will be who we are in eternity. We will not be different persons; we will be the same persons who have once and for all been redeemed, and who eternal existence will be in some way embodied. The New Testament does not teach a doctrine of the immaterial soul that goes off to heaven; rather it teaches resurrection—a redeemed bodily existence that we will enjoy on a new earth for all eternity (Revelation 21:1-5).

The bodily resurrection of Jesus is essential to Christian faith because it is God's affirmation that this world matters, that God intends to save this world and so it is critically important to seek justice in this life, to feed the poor in this life, and to care for the environment in this life. An early christological argument for the full humanity of Jesus was "that which he has not become he has not saved." In like fashion, that which Jesus has not overcome he has not defeated. If Jesus body remained dead, death is still in control and stalks us with no hope for victory. If Jesus' resurrection is simply a metaphor for his spirit rising to be with God, then salvation is nothing more than pie-in-the-sky in the sweet by-and-by. Such faith becomes other-worldly, divorced from the real problems of human existence that God desires to eliminate. When faith is divorced from history, it is divorced from the reality of this world; and when it is divorced from the reality of this world, all that matters is going to heaven when we die. We do not need to be concerned that the poor are fed; after all they will die soon enough and go to be with God. Those who care so much about justice in this world need to embrace the bodily raised Jesus. The reason why Paul and Timothy exhort the Colossians to live the resurrected life in the here and now is because what happens in the here and now matters to God; and we know it matters because he raised his Son, Jesus Christ from the dead.

CLOSING PRAYER

Gregory of Nazianzus (around 330-389) writes of Easter,

Today we rejoice in the salvation of the world.
Christ is risen; let us arise in him!
Christ enters new life; let us live in him;
Christ has come forth from the tomb;
let us shake off the fetters of evil!
The gates of hell are open,
the powers of evil are overcome!
In Christ a new creation is coming to birth,
Alleluia!
Lord, make us new,
Alleluia!

LESSON 7
LIVING IN THE CHRISTIAN HOUSEHOLD
(COLOSSIANS 3:18-4:1)

OBJECTIVE

In lesson seven our objective is four-fold: first, to understand Colossians 3:18-4:1, commonly called a household code in New Testament scholarship, in its first-century context, and highlight the Colossian house-code in its larger cultural and social context. Second, we must analyze the purpose and place of the house-code in the letter to the Colossians. Third, there must be some analysis on exactly how the Colossians are to behave in their various household roles—wives, husbands, fathers, children, slaves, and masters. Finally, we will ask how Colossians 3:18-4:1 speaks to Christian households in the twenty-first century—the household of the individual family unit and the household of the church.

OPENING PRAYER

As we begin to think of community and family relationships, let us be mindful as we pray of the families that are very broken and in need of healing and reconciliation.

> *Father of all humanity, make the roof of my house wide enough for all opinions, oil the door of my home so it opens easily to a friend and stranger and set such a table in my house that my whole family may speak kindly and freely around it.*[81]

---

81   Source unknown (Hawaii), *The Complete Book of Christian Prayer* (New York: Continuum, 1995), p. 74.

READING COLOSSIANS 3:18-4:1

Read this passage three times in three different translations taking note of the different words used as verbs in the passage. Highlight those words for discussion.

LESSON

INTRODUCTION

Paul's letter to the Colossians is not the only place in the New Testament in which readers encounter a household code. Such codes are found in Ephesians 5:22-6:9, Titus 2:1-10, 1 Peter 2:13-3:7, and various related verses in 1 Timothy: 2:1ff., 8ff.; 3:1ff., 8ff.; 5:17ff.; 6:1f. It is not our purpose to delve into the house-codes behind the texts other than Colossians. The only point to be made here is that if the New Testament is a judge by which we may draw a conclusion, household management and the roles of those in the household was a concern in the first-century church.

Many believers read the house-codes of the New Testament and find themselves bewildered. Why is slavery simply accepted as an institution? Why are wives subordinate to their husbands? Why doesn't Paul tell masters to release their slaves and husbands to treat their wives as equals. Judging from twenty-first century standards the household codes of the New Testament seem quite archaic.

In reading any ancient text, it is important that we not read our current context on to the ancient one. Paul and his contemporaries two thousand years ago lived in a world with such different customs and social contexts and political realities that it would be unfair to read our context onto theirs and conclude that they are deficient. It is also important that we do not simply dismiss our ancient descendants as primitive people who knew very little of the world and life compared to us. It is true that we know certain things they did not, but let's not fool ourselves into thinking that we have become so enlightened that we always know better than they. At this point, I would remind my readers that more blood has been spilled by war in the twentieth century than all the previous wars in all prior centuries combined and much of that has had nothing to do with religion. So much for enlightened ways of thinking.

So, if we want to hear Paul and Timothy's admonitions to Christians in first-century Asia Minor in reference to family relations, we need to hear them in their context. Otherwise we cannot know what we are to do with them today.

NEW TESTAMENT SCHOLARSHIP AND THE HOUSE-CODES IN THE LARGER CONTEXT

The concern for household management was very important in the ancient world. It was believed by the Romans that the family unit was the center and the foundation of the empire. If the family were to break down, so would the empire. New Testament scholar James D.G. Dunn makes five observations: First, household management was a common concern of Christians in the third and fourth generations and this concern centered around the relationships between husbands and wives, fathers and their children, and masters and their slaves. Second, there is no standard pattern being passed along, meaning there was no written form, a catechesis (introductory religious instruction), for example, from which the house-codes were drawn. Third, the three-fold pattern (husband/wife, father/child, master/slave) reflects the typical family structure of the time. Fourth, the household code undoubtedly reflects the patriarchal character of the first century CE. This cannot be denied, in spite of such passages as Colossians 3:19 and especially Ephesians 5:25-33. Such passages were meant to temper a husband's treatment of his wife. Egalitarian concerns were simply not in mind. The concern in the household was not equality but unity. Fifth, slaves were quite prominent in first century households, and were regarded as part of the household.[82]

---

82 Dunn, "The Household Rules in the New Testament," in S. Barton (ed.), *The Family in Theological Perspective* (Edinburgh: T & T Clark, 1996), pp. 43, 47-48.

Roman, Jewish, and Christian documents clearly reveal the general interest in household management. Seneca[83] is a fine example of the interest in these three paired relationships we find in Colossians. But it was not only the Greeks and the Romans who shared such concerns, Jews did as well. 9*Ps.-Phoc.* 175-227; Philo, *Hypothetica* 7.14; *Dec.* 165-167; *Spec. Leg.* 2.224-241; Josephus, *Apion* 2.199-208.) And so did Christians. (*Did.* 4.9-11; *1 Clement* 21.6-9; *Barnabas* 19.5-7; Polycarp *Philippians* 4.2-3; Ignatius, *Pol.* 4.1-5.2.) All these documents reflect varied interest in the three paired relationships of husband/wife, child/father, slave/master.

New Testament scholars have debated for decades whether the background of the New Testament household codes is primarily Roman, Jewish, or uniquely Christian. In one sense these three contexts all serve as the background for the house-codes because the good ordering of the household was of common concern in the first century world. On the other hand, there are really no precise parallels to the house-codes. It would be going too far to say that the New Testament house-codes are *uniquely* Christian, but it is in my view correct to say that the house-codes are decisively Christian in their concern that all believers in whatever station they may have in life act in a way that honors the Lord Jesus Christ whom they serve. I hope that will become clear in the pages below.

THE PURPOSE OF THE HOUSE-CODE AND ITS PLACE IN COLOSSIANS

As has been said, the major concern of the New Testament house-codes is the good management of the household. These households were no doubt diverse in reference to the level of Christian commitment among the family members. Some households might be entirely Christian while others might have only one or two followers of Jesus in the family. Nevertheless, Paul and Timothy have some instructions for how Christians are to behave toward others in the household in which they live.

83　*Epistulae* 94.1.

Early in the twentieth century, New Testament scholars were generally of the opinion that the concerns expressed in the Colossian house-code had very little if nothing to do with the interests of the rest of the letter. This meant that the house-code was independent from the rest of the letter. Paul and Timothy put it in there as an aside. The consensus of scholarship was that the first generation of Christians were expecting Jesus to return in their lifetime. As that generation aged and as second generation of Christians were now coming into their prime, the church had to contend with how to live in the world with the delay of the Christ's second coming. Faced with continued life in the world, the early Christians had to consider how they would live in their everyday relationships and affairs. The house-code was the result of that consideration. This view continues to have adherents even now in the early years of the twenty-first century. Petr Pokorný writes,

> The adoption of the household codes could not yet have taken place in the era of apocalyptic expectation of an imminent return during which the main letters of Paul were written.[84]

According to this particular view, the early church exchanged a neglect of concern over familiar relationships, since they were all coming to an end soon, for an orderly life in the world. It would have been quite natural, therefore, to take instruction in how to live in the world from that world. Thus, the older first generation of Christians and the younger second generation of Christians simply conformed their ethic making it conventional with the culture.[85]

This means two-things: First, the house-codes of the New Testament could only come about because of the receding expectations

---

84 Pokorný, *Colossians: A Commentary* (Peabody: Hendrickson, 1987), p. 177.

85 See Margaret MacDonald, *The Pauline Churches: A Social Historical Study of Institutionalization in the Pauline and Deutero-Pauline Writings* (Cambridge: Cambridge University Press, 1988), pp. 102-105.

of Christ's return; and second, the conventional cultural moral values of the house-code in Colossians meant that it had very little to nothing to do with the argument of the letter, except perhaps in a superficial way. The house-code in Colossians is nothing more than material addressing the common needs in broad circles of the earliest Christian communities.

I want to suggest that the belief that the Colossian house-code was the result of the delayed return of Jesus and that it has nothing to do with the larger context of the letter are simply mistaken.

It does appear to be the case that there were at least some Christians in the first generation who expected the imminent return of Jesus during their lives as seems to be the case in 2 Peter 3:3-4, but the situation in the early church was more complex than simply assuming the majority of the first Christians expected Christ to return soon. Indeed, it seems by the context of Colossians, the purpose of the house-code is not how Christians should live now that the end has been delayed, but rather how believers should live as citizens of the new age that has already dawned. We have seen throughout Colossians that the Christians are reminded that they are in Christ, and now in the Lord, which Paul reminds them of three times in the house-code, they are to live as citizens of the kingdom of God's beloved Son (1:12). The house-code in Colossians clarifies further in the letter how believers are to live in the dawn of the new age, not how one lives because of the failure of the new age to arrive.

Yet, it must also be said that the concern for good household management in the early church reflects, not only an interest in living in the already brought near in Christ, but it also reveals that the early Christians were well aware of the fact that the not yet of Christ's return had still to arrive. (This is quite different from a failure to arrive.) Thus the house-code in Colossians does betray to some extent a compromise with the form of the current age. Yet, accommodation does not adequately describe the character of 3:18-4:1. While the house-code expresses the concern over good household management, an interest shared in common with

Jews and Romans, the orientation by which the Colossian Christians order their households is the same as in every aspect of their lives—the foundation of the household is Jesus Christ, the Lord. All relationships in the household must be pleasing to him.

WIVES, HUSBANDS, CHILDREN, FATHERS, SLAVES, AND MASTERS

We begin this section by noting that the first century Greco-Roman and Jewish world was patriarchal, that is the head of the household was the man who was known in many households as husband, father, and master. He was to provide and to protect the household. Those who fell under his oversight in return for his care offered their submission and allegiance. Many Greeks and Romans believed that each person's station in life was according to the natural order. Thus, a slave should be a slave according to nature while women and men are also in roles destined for them.[86] What is important to note is that Paul and Timothy do not appeal to the natural order in the instructions to individual members of the household, nor do they suggest that slaves, for example, are slaves because they are fated to be. They accept that the household contains various roles as is, but their appeal to how each role is fulfilled is that which is fitting in the Lord.

The house-code in Colossians is not innovative in that it does not call for equality in the household, but it is "unsettling," as Richard Hays notes, because the head of the household (husband, father, and master) is admonished also to attend to his roles as is fitting in the Lord.[87] Thus, the head of the household may not treat the subordinate members in any way he sees fit. So, while the traditional roles are left in place, there is an attempt to reorder the household from within. It is a mistake to interpret this passage

---

86 Elisabeth Fiorenza, *In Memory of Her: A Feminist Reconstruction of Christian Origins* (Spring Valley: Crossroads, 1994), pp. 254-258.

87 Richard B. Hays, *The Moral Vision of the New Testament: A Contemporary Introduction to New Testament Ethics* (San Franciscom: Harper Collins, 1996), pp. 64-65.

in such a way that Paul and Timothy are seen as defenders of the patriarchal household, but neither are they out to destroy it, as if that were even an option in their context of the first-century Roman world.

Wives are told to be subordinate to their husbands. This admonition simply reflects Roman law. But it is important to note that what Paul and Timothy are insisting upon is subordination not subjugation. Thus, they tell the husbands to "love their wives and never treat them harshly" (3:19). Of course, there is nothing distinctively Christian about husbands loving their wives in the first century. Married relationships then as well as today were often quite loving. But "a distinctive Christian note"[88] can be heard in Paul's use of the term "love." The Greek verb is *agapaō*; the noun is *agapé*—the same word used by Jesus for the love shared by his disciples and the term used to refer to Christ's sacrificial self-giving on the cross. James Dunn states,

> The allusion to Christ as the model of love in action, it is true, did not alter the subordinate role attributed to the wife in 3:18, however, much it might have conditioned that role and prevented abuse of the power of the *paterfamilias* [the male head of the household]. But it does remain significant that the talk here is not of authority and rights but of obligations and responsibilities.[89]

The issue for Paul is not who has authoritative status in the household, but rather that all those who are "in Christ" live as those who are raised with Christ. This is true for the subordinates and the head of the house.

Children are the next subordinates charged. They are to obey their parents. Minor children old enough to understand Paul's words are likely in view here. Obedience includes respect and honor. And while the biblical commandment to honor father and

---

88   James D.G. Dunn, *The Epistles to the Colossians and Philemon* (Grand Rapids: Eerdmans, 1996), p. 248.
89   *Ibid*, p. 249.

mother (Exodus 20:12) was directed toward adult children honoring and taking care of the elderly parents, it was certainly expected in Judaism and Christianity that young children were to obey their parents. That children are told to obey assumes that the parents deal wisely and kindly with their children.

It must also be recognized that in Roman law, children were even more vulnerable than wives. They were considered the property of the father and thus in the eyes of the law were equivalent to the slaves of the household. It is important, therefore, to recognize Paul's charge to the fathers not to "provoke" their children so that they do not "lose heart" (3:21). Once again we see that the emphasis is not on the rights of the father given by Roman law, but on the responsibilities they have "in the Lord" as fathers to encourage their children, lest they become discouraged in their faith. Since the worshiping household is also in view here, Paul and Timothy could be encouraging the head of the household to give their children a role in worship instead of marginalizing them off to the side in silence. To encourage them to practice their faith along with the rest of the church is one way to build faith and a reminder that Jesus used a child as an example of the nature of God's kingdom (Matthew 19:13-15).

Finally, Paul addresses the slaves and the masters. Of first importance is the fact that the slaves themselves are addressed as responsible individuals. In much contemporary parallel literature, only the masters are addressed in advising them on how to handle their slaves.[90] But here the slaves are members of the church and are instructed directly in the same way the children are addressed. They are to be good slaves offering their service to the Lord. We hear in these verses an echo of 3:17 that whatever is done in word or deed is to be done in the "name of the Lord Jesus, giving thanks to God the Father through him." Whatever one's station in life, all of life is to be lived in a way that is pleasing to God. This means that their good behavior is not to be seen only to impress the master

---

90   Crouch, *Origin and Intention*, pp. 115-116.

only hoping to win his good favor. But their focus should be that all things are to be done for the Lord Jesus.

The head of the household is addressed for the third time as "master." Masters too have responsibilities toward their slaves. As the slaves are to be conscientious in reference to their work, so the master must treat their slaves "justly and fairly." It is striking that these two terms could be used in reference to the law itself. If so then what Paul and Timothy might be suggesting is that slaves should be treated in the community of faith by the same standard as everyone else. Thus while the slave remains a slave, in the Christian household they are judged by the same standard as everyone else in the household. Such instruction would give practical force to 3:11 where Paul insists that the renewal in Christ's means that there was no "slave and free." In the eyes of Roman law slaves remain slaves and masters remain masters, in Christ there is a reordering taking place in the household itself.

In order to reinforce to the masters the importance of how they treat their slaves, Paul issues a warning to them— "for you know that you have a master in heaven" (4:1). The last verse of chapter 3 reminds the slaves of their responsibility to live with integrity as far as it depends upon them to do so, but it also reassures them that God, the heavenly master, will judge the master of the household by the same standard by which they judge their slaves.

A First-Century Reality and a Twenty-First Century Question

I return to some perplexing realities I mentioned above that we twenty-first century Christians have with this material. One of the questions often raised when reading the house-codes of the New Testament is why did Paul just accept the subordination of wives as a given? Why does he accept slavery as the reality? If in Jesus Christ there is truly no slave and free, why not tell the masters of the household to release their slaves?

While such questions are understandable in the twenty-first century, they don't take into account the very different world Paul and Timothy lived in that simply cannot be compared to today. First of all, it must be said that for most of human history women have been viewed as subordinate to men. The idea that they are completely equal is rather new. In the United States women weren't given the right to vote until 1920, and didn't turn out to vote in equal numbers until 1980.[91] So, before we are too hard on the writers of Colossians, we would do well to remember our recent history.

In reference to slaves, I quote James D.G. Dunn,

> Christians who wanted as much freedom as possible within these structures to pursue a Christian calling as members of the church were wise to carry out their responsibilities as slaves with all diligence. This should not be criticized as merely social conformism; those who live in modern social democracies, in which interest groups can hope to exert political pressure by intensive lobbying, should remember that in the cities of Paul's day the great bulk of Christians would have had no possibility whatsoever of exerting any political pressure for any particular policy and reform. In such circumstances a pragmatic quietism was the most effective means of gaining room enough to develop the quality of personal relationship which would establish and build up the microcosms (churches) of transformed communities.[92]

It would never have occurred to Paul and Timothy to petition Rome for an end to slavery. That was not the world in which they lived. But the new world in Jesus Christ invited and challenged the first-century Christians to reorder their lives according to that new creation, while having to exist in the old order that was now passing away and would one day cease to exist. "Ordinary tasks are placed in a different interpretive framework."[93] They were to live as

---

91   http://www.history.com/topics/womens-history/the-fight-for-womens-suffrage.

92   James D.G. Dunn, *The Epistles to the Colossians and Philemon* (Grand Rapids: Eerdmans, 1996), p. 253.

93   Charles H. Talbert, *Ephesians and Colossians* (Grand Rapids: Baker Academic, 2007), p. 234.

kingdom citizens because Jesus was Lord even though Caesar still claimed to be the measure of all things.

I dare say Christians have the same challenge in the twenty-first century.

Discussion Questions

1. In the nineteenth century Christians in the United States would use the New Testament house-codes to justify the institution of slavery. Looking at the house-codes in their context, we now know that the situation of the first-century Christians was very different from Christians living in a modern democracy with the right to petition the government. No one in the know would use these texts to keep human beings in bondage today. What other biblical passages might we be reading without knowledge of the context to justify certain practices today?

2. Today there are Christians that have used the New Testament house-codes to argue that the husband today should still be the head of the household and the wife should be subordinate. The problem with that view is that it fails to take into account the first century Roman context in which a patriarchal household was a given that could not be changed. Moreover, it misses the larger theological implications of Paul instructing the husbands to love their wives. In Ephesians, Paul is very clear as to what such love means. Husbands are to love their wives as Christ loved the church and gave himself up for her (Ephesians 4:25). While Paul is not promoting equality in either letter, we see a theological trajectory toward equality. For husbands to love their wives as Christ loved the church is to love them sacrificially, and deny themselves for their wives' sake. Here we see a glimpse of mutual submission in the Christian household. Do you think this suggestion is correct? In the Christian household today, should mutual submission be the rule?

3. What does it mean to do all things "in the Lord?" Are there times when that motivation is unrealistic in the world in which we live?

EXERCISE

Spend some time reflecting on your family relationships. Do those relationships reflect what is fitting in the Lord? If there is any family member that you have behaved toward in less than a Christian way, consider approaching that person and asking for forgiveness. List some ways you can be in service to your family in a way that would be pleasing to Christ.

HISTORICAL/THEOLOGICAL REFLECTION

In his book, *The Politics of Jesus*, John Howard Yoder refers to the New Testament house-codes as promoting "revolutionary subordination." He writes,

> The liberation of the Christian from "the way things are," which has been brought about by the gospel of Christ, who freely took upon himself the bondages of history in our place, is so thorough and novel as to make evident to the believer that the givenness of his subjection to the enslaving or alienating powers of this world is broken. It is natural to feel Christ's liberation reaching into every kind of bondage, and to want to act in accordance with that radical shift.
>
> His [Jesus'] motto of revolutionary subordination, of willing servanthood in the place of domination, enables the person in a subordinate position in society to accept and live within that status without resentment, at the same time that it calls upon the person in the superordinate position to forsake or renounce all domineering use of his status.... The claim is not that there is immediately a new world regime which violently replaces the old: but rather the old and the new order exist concurrently on different levels.
>
> Since in the resurrection and in Pentecost the kingdom which was imminent has now in part come into our history, the church can now live out, within the structures of society,

the newness of the life of that kingdom....The wife or the child or slave who can accept subordination because "it is fitting in the Lord" has not forsaken the radicality of the call of Jesus; it is precisely this attitude toward the structures of the world, this freedom from needing to smash them since they about to crumble anyway, which Jesus had been the first to teach and in his suffering to concretize (pp. 189-190, 191, 192).

CLOSING PRAYER

Let us offer this prayer for our families:

> *Heavenly Father, please shine your light upon my family. Give us strength to overcome all of the difficulties that we are dealing with now and protect us against any and all problems we may encounter in the future. O Lord, please bring us together as we are meant to be. May the love that binds us only grow stronger as we fulfill the destiny you have laid out for us.*
>
> *Grant my family forgiveness for any sins we have committed. May we also forgive one another Lord, as it is sometimes difficult to do.*
>
> *Bless us Lord, In your name I pray, Amen.*[94]

---

94   "Prayers for Special Help," http://www.prayers-for-special-help. com/prayer-for-family.html.

Lesson 8
Final Instructions, Greetings, and Benediction (Colossians 4:2-18)

Objective

In this final lesson as Paul closes his letter to the church, he engages in some brief final instruction, and greetings of specific people. We will be reminded that the church of the first century was made of up real and living people, a community faithful to its mission and also in need of reminders. Their mission two thousand years ago is the same as ours today—to make disciples of Jesus. They had their time in this world, and now is our time. We cannot be faithful without the faithfulness of those who went before.

Opening Prayer

> *Almighty God,*
> *you have knit together your elect*
> *in one communion and fellowship,*
> *in the mystical body of your Son Christ our Lord.*
> *Grant us grace*
> *so to follow your holy saints in all virtuous and godly living,*
> *that we may come to those unspeakable joys,*
> *which you have prepared for those who sincerely love you;*
> *through Jesus Christ our Lord. Amen.*[95]

---

95 *The United Methodist Hymnal* (1989) #713.

READING COLOSSIANS 4:2-18

Read 4:2-18 three times taking note of what Paul says about each individual mentioned. What questions do you have about each person? What is left unsaid that peaks your curiosity?

LESSON

FINAL INSTRUCTIONS

Paul and Timothy offer some final instructions to the Colossians, some of it by way of reminder that was written earlier. First, the Colossians are to devote themselves to prayer. As Paul remembers the Colossians in prayer continually—he thanks God for the Colossians (1:3) and he prays for their faithfulness (1:9), so the Colossians are to pray as well. They too are to offer thanksgiving, a theme already referred to (also 1:12; 2:7; 3:17), and they are to pray for Paul and his missionary work, specifically that an opportunity will present itself to "declare the mystery of Christ." Paul's reference to the door opening to the possibility of preaching could very well be a not-so-veiled reference to his imprisonment, which has hindered his evangelistic work. Thus, Paul is asking the Colossians to pray for his release. The irony is that it was precisely Paul's preaching that put him in prison in the first place. As one not to be detoured from his calling, he is asking that he will be freed so he can resume the work that got him arrested. Paul's main concern does not seem to be his freedom in and of itself, but that his freedom is necessary to continue his work. Paul is singularly focused on the calling he received on the Damascus Road many years before (Acts 9:1-19).

The substance of his message is the "mystery of Christ" which Paul and Timothy refer to in 1:25-27—that is, that the gospel, the Good News of salvation in Jesus Christ has now been made available to the Gentiles. All persons have been extended the invitation. In verse 4 Paul asks the Colossians to pray for Paul that he may have the courage to preach in difficult circumstances. He also refers to his message as being revealed affirming once again that his gospel is of divine origin (1:25-27; see also Galatians 1:11-12).[96]

This short section on further instructions continues to focus on the concern of evangelism, but not in the use of words alone, but also in conduct. The Colossians are to act wisely toward those outside the church, those outside the faith. The house-code and its call for unity in the household may likely serve an apologetic purpose. A well-run and responsible and loving household could serve as a witness to unbelievers so that they might become receptive to hearing the gospel. But acting wisely toward unbelievers is something that informs all of life. Even though Paul has been treated terribly by outsiders who put him in prison, his charge to the Christians at Colossae hardly reflects a vindictive attitude. David Hay writes,

> Despite the suggestion of hostility on the part of outsiders in Paul's reference to imprisonment (v. 3), the tone of verses 5-6 is irenic and nondefensive. Christians are understood to live in a realm of "light" sharply separated from the "darkness" of the non-Christian world (1:13); and those outside the light realm face condemnation (3:6). Yet the boundary line can always be crossed. There is no difference toward, or hatred of, those outside. Church members are enjoined to communicate effectively and appropriately with non-Christians, though the form of their witness is expected to be different from that of "professional" missionaries like Paul.[97]

Some have suggested that Paul's reference to "making most of the time" in verse 5 may refer to Paul's belief that Christ's return was imminent, and that the Colossians should not trifle away their time in endeavors that do not further the mission. We cannot say for sure; it is certainly the case that Christ's return will happen only in the timeline of God the Father, (Matthew 24:36), so making the most of the days and years given to Jesus' followers is true in every

---

96   Jerry L. Sumney, *Colossians A Commentary* (Louisville: WJKP, 2008), p. 259.

97   David M. Hay, *Colossians* (Nashville: Abingdon, 2000), pp. 152-153.

generation. Jesus may return at any moment, but even if does not in our generation, we still need to remain focused on our mission because one lifetime, no matter how long, is still very brief.

Paul clarifies how the Colossians are to behave toward unbelievers, particularly in conversation. Their words are to be "gracious" and "seasoned with salt." Such a way of conversing may serve the purpose of diffusing any hostility those outside the church may have for the Christians. For language to be seasoned with salt is not uniquely Christian, and should not be confused with what we mean today when we refer to someone's language as salty. The expression is reminiscent of Jesus who referred to his followers as "the salt of the earth" (Matthew 5:13) and could be in Paul's mind. The Greek historian, Plutarch, a younger contemporary of Paul writes in his treatise, On Talkativeness 654F, that those speaking can express "a certain grace by means of words as with salt." He also says elsewhere, "For wit is probably the tastiest condiment of all. Therefore, some call it 'graciousness' because it makes the necessary chore of eating pleasant" (Moralia 685A).[98]

Words seasoned with salt are non-defensive, humorous, and gracious. How pleasurable it is to engage someone in conversation whose words fit this description. How something is said is just as important as what is said.

GREETINGS

Paul and Timothy now offer greetings from specific individuals in their mission. Such good wishes at the end of a letter was common in the ancient world, and was used by Paul elsewhere (see Romans 16:1-16 and 1 Corinthians 16:13-20).

Three times Paul mentions Tychicus and Onesimus who have been entrusted to take this letter to the Colossians. They will inform the Colossians of Paul's situation in prison upon their arrival. It was likely the case that Paul had much more personal information he wanted to convey to the Colossians, but felt he could not do so in

---

98   See Ben Witherington III, *The Letters to Philemon, the Colossians, and the Ephesians* (Grand Rapids: Eerdmans, 2007), pp. 199-200.

letter form. It was also possible that Paul did not want to say too much about his situation that would be read by his captors and perhaps hurt Paul's hope of release.

Paul refers to Tychicus and Onesimus as "beloved brothers." Tychicus is mentioned in Ephesians 6:21-22 and is listed as a co-worker. His affection for both men and their common work in the Lord are indispensable to Paul. The Onesimus referred to here is the slave Onesimus referred to in Philemon. Paul refers to Onesimus as "one of you." He is returning home, perhaps also bearing the letter Paul wrote to Philemon, who owns Onesimus. It is important to note that nowhere does Paul refer to Onesimus as a slave in Colossians. We only know this from Philemon. Perhaps this reflects Paul's understanding of Onesimus' new status in Christ that he is "no longer a slave but more than a slave—a beloved brother" (Philemon 16).

Aristarchus appears to be in prison with Paul. In Acts 19:29, he is identified as being from Thessalonica and was with Paul in the riot in Ephesus (Acts 19:21-41). Some have suggested that the phrase "fellow prisoner" is more of a title Paul gives to designate Aristarchus as a "captive of Christ,"[99] but since Paul is indeed in prison at the time of the writing of this letter, and that he refers to no one else in this way, suggests that Aristarchus was an actual prisoner in chains with Paul.

Mark, the cousin of Barnabas, is mentioned next. This reference is interesting for two reasons: First, Mark is identified as Barnabas' cousin, which helps to illuminate Acts 15:36-41 where Barnabas and Paul have a sharp disagreement over whether or not to take Mark with them on a tour back to the cities where they had already preached. Paul did not want to take Mark because Mark had left them for an unknown reason at an earlier time. Barnabas' kinship with Mark led him to intercede for his cousin, but to no avail. The argument led to a split in their missionary work—Barnabas took Mark, and Paul partnered with Silas.

---

99   See David E. Garland, *Colossians/Philemon* (Grand Rapids: Zondervan, 1998), p. 277.

Second, the fact that Mark is now with Paul in Colossae some years later means that there was a reconciliation between the two men. Once again they were in mission together. Those who preach the reconciliation offered in Jesus Christ, need to be reconciled to one another if the work is to go on.

The trio of Jewish Christians there with Paul is complete with the mention of "Jesus who is called Justus" (4:11). It was not uncommon for Jews to take a second Greek or Latin name that would be easier to pronounce in the Roman world (see Acts 1:23; 13:9; 18:7). Taking such a name might also be a way a Jew might hope to avoid discrimination by Gentiles.

Aristarchus, Mark, and Justus are the only co-workers who are "of the circumcision." If the problem the Colossians face is critique from the Jews of the synagogue in Colossae, perhaps Paul is reminding them that there are Jews who have become followers of Jesus. There were indeed persons from Paul's "kindred" (cf. Romans 9:1-5) that had embraced the gospel.

Epaphras, like Onesimus, is identified as "one of you" (4:12), suggesting his geographical origins. Paul refers to him as a servant of Christ Jesus, but not as a fellow prisoner. He is a prayer-warrior on the Colossians' behalf. The NRSV states that Epaphras is always "wrestling" in prayer, but the Greek word (*agonizomai*) can also be rendered as "struggle," or "agonize," the same way Jesus prayed in the Garden of Gethsemane (Luke 22:43-44).

Luke and Demas are mentioned last. It is only here in Colossians that Luke is described as a physician. While there is no specific mention anywhere in the New Testament that Luke was a Gentile, since Paul does not count him among "the circumcision" with him, his Gentile status is clearly implied. We get no details about Demas, but he is mentioned in 2 Timothy 4:10 as having abandoned Paul on account of his love for the "present world."

Finally, Paul turns his greetings outward to other Christians. He greets the sisters and brothers in Laodicea, which appears to be strange since this letter is addressed to the Colossians. But in 4:17, Paul instructs the Colossians to take this letter to Laodicea read it to the church there after it is read to the Colossians. The greetings make sense, therefore, in that context. The perplexing question, however, is why would Paul not greet the Laodiceans in the letter written to them?

It must be noted that Paul does not refer to the Laodicean letter as *to* the Laodiceans; rather he mentions the letter that comes *from* Laodicea. I have suggested elsewhere that the book of Ephesians is the letter Paul refers to as from Laodicea.[100] Two reasons will suffice: First, it appears that Ephesians was written as a circular letter written to the churches of Asia Minor. The phrase "in Ephesus" in Ephesians 1:1 does not appear in the earlier manuscripts. As a circular letter its final destination may have been Ephesus—hence the connection with that city. In addition, there are no personal greetings in Ephesus, which is very strange considering that Paul spent a fair amount of time with the church there. If Ephesians is the letter Paul is referring to, a general letter to several congregations would contain no personal greetings at the end. So, it could be that Paul wrote Colossians with his specific concerns to the church there and greeting the Laodiceans in the letter knowing that it was going directly to Laodicea. After Colossians was composed, Paul then decided to write a general letter to the churches in Asia Minor reemphasizing in a general way, his concern over the universal nature of the gospel. That letter is our book of Ephesians in the New Testament. The Jewish and Gentile concerns in the first-century church were wrestled over for years and they were hardly isolated to one city.

In 4:15 Nympha is mentioned and the church in her house. In comparing New Testament manuscripts, it is not clear whether Nympha should be Nymphas—a man. Most scholars have decided in favor of Nympha being a woman. If so, it would mean that a church was meeting in her house, and that perhaps she was its head being single or widowed. If there is more than one house church in

---

100 Allan R. Bevere, "The *Cheiropgraph* in Colossians 2:14 and the Ephesian Connection," in B.J. Oropeza, et al. eds. *Jesus and Paul* (London: T & T Clark, 2009), pp. 199-206.

Laodicea, it is significant that Paul singles out her and the church in her house for mention. Perhaps she is a well respected Christian leader.

Finally, Archippus is mentioned briefly and in a way that can be considered a word of warning or encouragement. If Paul has in mind the kind of reminder he issues to Timothy in 2 Timothy 4:5, then Paul is offering a word of encouragement.

BENEDICTION

Paul and Timothy close their letter with a final hand-written greeting, a plea to remember his situation in prison, and a final benediction.

It was common for the writer of a letter dictating or outlining it to a secretary to personally sign the letter, giving its words authority and authenticity. We cannot know Paul's situation in prison. If Timothy is the one who actually penned the letter, perhaps Paul outlined his general concerns to Timothy, and Timothy wrote the letter giving it his own style and flair. Paul upon hearing the finished product read to him in prison, then signed off on the letter giving it his stamp of approval. It is unknown as to the kind of license Paul gave to his secretaries. Since Romans is considered to be written in Pauline style, it may be the secretary writing that letter, Tertius, (Romans 16:22) was simply writing word for word what Paul was dictating to him. Given the different style of Colossians, it may be that Paul was unable to have that kind of direct input. Thus, Timothy had to write the letter in his own style and verbiage after consulting with Paul. Colossians is nevertheless, Pauline—so-much-so that Paul signed off giving it his authority.

Paul ends with the typical benediction wishing God's grace to the Colossians. God is the giver and sustainer of grace. Jesus' followers are to demonstrate that divine grace in their lives. In so doing, they offer the presence of God to others. Paul's chains do not raise questions about God's grace in Paul's life; rather they are a reminder to Paul of the grace of God that called him to preach the gospel. It is God's grace that liberated Paul whether he is in prison or free to travel. As Paul said to King Agrippa, "Except for these chains, I wish you become as I am" (Acts 26:29).

DISCUSSION QUESTIONS

1. Prayer is an indispensable practice in the Christian life. It is not a practice reserved for pastors, or missionaries, or those persons in the church that we perceive to be super-spiritual. All of us are to pray. How is your prayer life? How often do you pray? Does your prayer life need improvement?
2. It is clear from reading Paul's final instructions and his greetings that his mission was a team effort. God does not intend for us to go it alone as Christians. We need to be together for the sake of our individual spiritual growth and we cannot make disciples of Jesus Christ without the teamwork of the church. Where do you see the teamwork of your church contributing to God's kingdom in the world?
3. Paul was singularly focused on his mission of proclaiming the gospel. He wouldn't even let his imprisonment distract him from his central and all-encompassing purpose in life. What distracts us today from being God's people in the way God wants us to be? Have we allowed ourselves to become distracted from the mission Jesus has given us as his disciples?

EXERCISE

If you have never done so, consider keeping a daily prayer journal. Write down your praises and concerns each day as you go to prayer. Keep track of what prayers are answered and how they are answered. We must always remember that God will often answer our prayers in his way, not ours. Also consider joining a prayer group at church. If there is no such group, consider starting one by enlisting persons in your church who pray regularly.

HISTORICAL/THEOLOGICAL REFLECTION

The second century *Epistle to Diogenes* represents a perspective similar in context to its presentation of the new life in Christ that puts believers in a new world, while being in mission to the current age.

> For Christians are not distinguished from the rest of humanity by country, language or custom. For nowhere do they live in cities of their own, nor do they speak some unusual dialect, nor do they practice an eccentric way of life. This teaching of theirs has not been discovered by the thoughts and reflection of ingenious people, nor do they promote any human doctrine, as some do. But while they live in both Greek and barbarian cities, as each one's lot was cast, and follow the local customs in dress and food and other aspects of life, at the same time they demonstrate the remarkable and admittedly unusual character of their own citizenship. They live in their own countries, but only as nonresidents; they participate in everything as citizens, and endure everything as foreigners. Every foreign country is their fatherland, and every fatherland is foreign.... They are in the flesh, but they do not live according to the flesh. They live on earth, but their citizenship is in heaven.[101]

CLOSING PRAYER

> *O Lord Jesus Christ, who at your first coming did send your messenger to prepare the way before you: grant that the ministers and stewards of your mysteries may likewise so prepare and make ready your way, by turning the hearts of the disobedient to the wisdom of the just, that at your second coming to judge the world we may be found an acceptable people in your sight; who lives and reigns with the Father and the Holy Spirit, ever one God, world without end.*[102]

---

101 *Diogenes*, 5.1-5,8-9; Quoted in Charles H. Talbert, *Ephesians and Colossians* (Grand Rapids: Baker Academic, 2007), pp. 238-239.
102 John Cosin, (1595-1672), *The Complete Book of Christian Prayer* (New York: Continuum, 1995), p. 445.

PHILEMON

LESSON 1

PHILEMON IN CONTEXT (PHILEMON 1-3)

OBJECTIVE

This first lesson will set the little letter of Philemon in its first century context. Participants will have a basic understanding of the epistle and major persons involved in the writing and the reading of the letter. Participants will also appreciate the important relationship between Paul, Philemon, and Onesimus that they have in Christ, that makes it possible for them to speak the truth in love to one another. Emphasis will be placed on the communal significance of the Christian life and how individual Christians should be mutually accountable to one another for the credibility of the church's witness in the world.

OPENING PRAYER

Dear God, Lover of us all, do not let me go down to the grace with old broken friendships unresolved. Give to us and to all with whom we have shared our lives and deepest selves along the Way, the courage not only to express anger when we feel let down, but your more generous love which always seeks to reconcile and so to build a more enduring love between those we have held dear as friends. Amen.[103]

---

103 Kathy Keay, *The Complete Book of Christian Prayer* (New York: Continuum, 1995), p. 84, 222.

READING PHILEMON 1-3

Read the first three verses of the letter several times in a translation of your choice. Focus particularly on the names mentioned. They were the names of people just like us who lived and breathed, laughed and cried some two thousand years ago. And just like us, they followed Jesus Christ as their Lord and Savior. As you read these verses try to imagine the house church hearing this letter read for the first time as they gathered together to worship.

In addition, read articles on "Philemon" and "slavery" in a Bible Dictionary.

LESSON

WHO WROTE PHILEMON?

Like the epistle to the Colossians, Philemon is written by Paul along with Timothy, Paul's traveling companion. If you will recall, I suggested that because the written style of Colossians was so different from what is referred to as Paul's undisputed letters—Romans, 1 and 2 Corinthians, Galatians, Philippians, and 1 Thessalonians—Timothy could very well have been the one who penned Colossians, perhaps because Paul was unable to do so in prison, or maybe he wanted to focus more on his letter to Philemon, allowing Timothy to outline his concerns to the Colossians. The letter to Philemon, however, is clearly written in the style of St. Paul. Perhaps this letter was short enough for Paul to manage in his bondage, or perhaps Paul dictated it to a secretary in the way he could not or did not with Colossians. In any case, Paul is indeed the author with Timothy acknowledged as Paul's missionary companion.

WHO WERE THE RECIPIENTS?

There are four recipient listed in verses one and two: ` 1) "Philemon, our dear friend and co-worker," 2) "to Apphia, our sister," 3) "to Archippus our fellow soldier," and 4) "to the church in your" [Philemon's] "house."

Since Philemon is mentioned first, he is the main person being addressed as is clearly indicated throughout the letter. Philemon was likely a man of some financial means.[104] Onesimus is his slave, and he may not be the only one in the household. Philemon hosts a church in his house, which may suggest that the home was larger and could accommodate such a gathering (the first century church was a house church movement). Paul refers to him as a "dear friend" (brother), which means that the two men had possibly built a deep friendship as one of Paul's fellow co-workers in the mission of Christ. But if that were the case, the two men would have had to work together outside of Colossae for Paul does not indicate that he has ever been there, and both his letters—Colossians and Philemon—indicate he had never visited. It is also possible that the two men never met, but know each other by reputation. More on these possibilities will be discussed at the appropriate time. Philemon was probably a man of some standing and well-respected—which may explain some of the language of Paul's appeal to him in the letter.

It is reasonable to assume that Apphia is Philemon's wife. While wives had no legal status, according to Roman law, in reference to managing the household, nevertheless, wives were responsible for managing the affairs of the household according to the husband's wishes. Thus, the matter concerning Onesimus' status as a slave would have been of concern to Apphia.[105] It is a courtesy to her that Paul includes her in the salutation.

Many have concluded that Archippus is the son of Philemon and Apphia. That could well have been the case, but we do not know for sure. Being referred to as "our fellow soldier," (*sustratiótés*) may indicate he is actively involved in the ministry of the house church, which is why he is specifically mentioned. Paul uses the same term in Philippians for Epaphroditus who is also referred to as a co-worker (2:25). So, Archippus may not be related by blood

---

104 For more on Philemon, see Marianne Meye Thompson, *Colossians and Philemon* (Grand Rapids: Eerdmans, 2005), p. 208.
105 David E. Garland, *Colossians/Philemon*, (Grand Rapids: Zondervan, 1998), p. 317.

to Philemon and Apphia, but he is related in Christ and in the common cause of the gospel.

Finally, the letter is addressed to the church in Philemon's house. It may seem strange to modern Western minds that Paul seems to be making the relationship between Philemon and Onesimus a public matter. In the twenty-first century we are so imbued in a hyper individualistic context that it's hard for us to understand why such matters should not be private. It is important to realize that Paul and his contemporaries did not have such an individualistic notion of privacy that we do today. To be sure, they understood that there were matters of a personal nature, but they rightly knew that even personal matters could affect the larger community. Since Philemon's household and his house church are so intertwined, Paul seems to assume that the situation with Onesimus is a concern of the entire house church. For Paul and the first-century Christians, church was family. Nowhere does Paul appeal to the congregation to make the decision on what to do with Onesimus, that decision is left to Philemon alone. But the public nature of the discussion would have put more pressure on Philemon to submit to Paul's request. It could also have been the case that if Onesimus were a runaway slave, that would not only have disrupted the household, but also the house church. Thus, Onesimus may have needed to be forgiven and restored to the fellowship.[106]

In verse 3 Paul offers a greeting typical of all his letters. The word "grace" is a reminder of God's initiative in the lives of believers, that salvation is indeed a gift from God. To wish peace (Hebrew *shalom*) is not simply to hope for the absence of conflict, but rather refers to a flourishing in all areas of life. It is holistic in its scope.

Such grace and peace comes from the "God and Father of our Lord Jesus Christ." God bestowed them on the church at the beginning, and they continue to need such blessings from God to continue in their service.

---

106 David E. Garland, *Colossians/Philemon* (Grand Rapids: Zondervan, 1998), p. 318.

Why Was the Letter Written?

The central purpose of the letter is one of intercession. Paul writes to Philemon to advocate on behalf of Philemon's slave Onesimus. The situation between Philemon and Onesimus is not completely clear. Why was Onesimus with Paul? Did he run away from his master? Was he sent to Paul by Philemon, but wronged his master in some other way(v. 18)? The vast majority of commentators take the position that Onesimus was indeed a runaway, but if so why seek out Paul to ask Philemon to take him back without consequences. Presumably a slave was running away because he did not wish to be a slave. James Dunn offers a possible solution. Onesimus was not a runaway slave, but a slave who left specifically to seek out Paul to intercede for him in another matter between him and his master.

> ... Onesimus left his house with the express purpose of contacting Paul. It was in fact quite a common occurrence at this time for a slave who had put himself in the wrong with his master in some way to seek out a friendly third party to ask the latter to plead on his behalf with his offended master. Where the slave's goal was not to run away but to restore effective working relations with his master, legal opinion did not regard him as a *fugitivus* [fugitive].[107]

If Dunn is correct then even though Philemon and Onesimus are master and slave, Paul truly becomes a third party mediator. What makes the situation even more dynamic is that Onesimus appears to accept Christ while with Paul. It thus becomes a "game-changer" in their relationship as Paul indicates to Philemon in verses 11 and 16. That makes it more understandable why the letter is also addressed to the church in Philemon's house. If Onesimus left Philemon as an unbeliever and now returns as a believer, he too is a member of the spiritual family that gathers for worship and prayer.

---

107 James D.G. Dunn, *The Epistles to the Colossians and Philemon* (Grand Rapids: Eerdmans, 1996), p. 304.

DISCUSSION QUESTIONS

1. Worship and fellowship in a diverse household like Philemon's was probably very challenging at times with people in the culturally defined roles, but also as Christians relating to one another as brothers and sisters in faith. What are some of their interesting dynamics you have encountered in your church family? What challenges do you face as a diverse church with a single mission?
2. Paul makes the situation between Onesimus and Philemon a public church matters. In a world of rampant individualism and "Lone Ranger" Christians, how does the church begin to move toward mutual accountability? Why is mutual accountability important? What are the potential pitfalls in attempting such accountability?

EXERCISE

If you are not part of a Christian accountability group, consider starting one. If there is no such ministry in your church, perhaps you can speak to your pastor about the need for one. A good resource to get started is Kevin Watson's little book, *The Class Meeting: Reclaiming a Forgotten (and Essential) Small Group Experience*. Seedbed, 2013.

HISTORICAL/THEOLOGICAL REFLECTION

Too many people today have the very mistaken view that it is possible to be a Christian without the church. All that matters is that one believes in Jesus. Unfortunately, such a view is not surprising in a culture like ours that put the individual as the primary moral agent. Such a context has trouble making sense of Paul's seeming assumption that the situation between Philemon and Onesimus is a matter for the entire church. But for the New Testament and for most of church history, the church has been viewed as indispensable to the Christian life. Jesus and the church go together.

The frustration people face is that all too often the church doesn't really look too much like Jesus. It is frail and fallible and everyone who has been associated with any church can tell stories of the church behaving badly.

There's an old story that I and more than a few preachers have used in a sermon at one time or another—that Noah's Ark was not a very pleasant place to be during the flood with the smelly animals and the stale air and being cooped up with no place to go. But as difficult as it must have been for Noah and his family, the Ark was still the best thing afloat at the time.

It is an obvious observation—the church is far from perfect. That is not an excuse; it is just a fact. And while we the church need to be going on to perfection, such perfection continues to elude us this side of the Second Coming. The church is a very leaky boat.

Like many others, I have been very critical of the church at times. We do not point out the church's failings because we hate the Body of Christ; on the contrary, we love it, and we know that if we are to faithfully follow Jesus, we need it. If we didn't love the church, we wouldn't care enough to raise the concerns we encounter.

To be part of the Church of Jesus Christ can be a very frustrating experience for all of us who are individual members of Christ's Body. I can list my reasons why I get so frustrated on occasion and so can many others. Some of those reasons are similar, others may be very different. There has been much talk about the church and how it has turned off the younger generation and how others who were very involved have given up on "organized religion." These concerns are legitimate and should be discussed with compassion and vigor and critical reflection.

But it serves no constructive purpose to focus only on the church's frailties and foibles ... though they seem to be many at times. What I would like to do is remind us that the church is not only an all-too-human institution, but it is a creation of God and brought into existence by the death and resurrection of Jesus Christ and through the life-giving breath of the Holy Spirit.

We must never forget that Jesus told his original disciples and, therefore, all of us who are disciples, that the gates of hell would not overcome the church (Matthew 16:18). I have often pondered the image offered to us by the Apostle Paul that the church is the Body of Christ (1 Corinthians 12:12-30), that the church is Christ's presence in a special redemptive way that cannot be seen anywhere else. In the church, God's kingdom ushered into the world and established by Jesus continues even today. And such work can be found in no other institution. If Jesus is the very presence of God in this world, then in a very real sense the church is the very presence of Christ in the world. But we must remember that unlike Jesus, who was sinless, the church consists of disciples, who are sinners, but hopefully going on to perfection... the emphasis in this context is "going on."

There are times when I am very discouraged with the church for various reasons. And on such occasions, it is helpful for me to remember that the church has struggled from the very beginning. In the Book of Acts after the wonderful event of Pentecost and the coming of the Holy Spirit and the Birthday of the Church, God's creation (Acts 2), it doesn't take too long before there is disagreement and fighting in the ranks (Acts 6). In other words, the church in the twenty-first century is not facing any more difficulties, any further disagreements, any more intense strife than what our Christian sisters and brothers faced in the first century. God, who always works in the context of the human situation has created and called a people to be his presence in the world. God has been more than willing for that presence to be imperfect; for even, and especially, in the church's imperfection, God can reveal God's grace.

One of the early symbols of the church is a boat in the midst of troubled seas. And while that image is meant to primarily convey the church staying afloat though tossed to and fro by worldly challenges and threats, it must also be remembered that the church continues to stay afloat and continues to stay on divine course even though the deck hands at times struggle and fight with one another. The captain of the ship, Jesus Christ, insures that nothing—threats from without and strife from within—will steer the church off its divinely appointed course and one day into the safe harbor of eternity.

We need Jesus and we need the church... and we cannot have one without the other.

And I will say this-- in spite of its foibles and frailties, there can be no kingdom work without the church, there can be no resurrection without the People of the Resurrection, there can be no Easter without Easter people to sing the praises of new life; without the church, there is no kingdom.

Yes, indeed... the church is one leaky boat... but it is indeed the best thing afloat.

CLOSING PRAYER

> *Most gracious Father, we humbly ask you for your holy universal Church. fill it with all truth; in all truth with all peace. Where it is corrupt, purify it; where it is in error direct it; where anything is amiss, reform it; where it is right, strengthen and confirm it; where it is in want, furnish it; where it is divided and rent asunder, make up the fissures of it, O holy on of Israel. Amen.*[108]

---

108 (Archbishop) Bull, 1571-1645 (adapted) *The Complete Book of Christian Prayer* (New York: Continuum, 1995), p. 429, 1085.

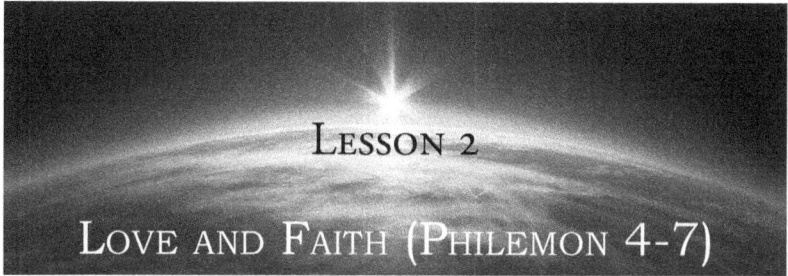

LESSON 2

LOVE AND FAITH (PHILEMON 4-7)

OBJECTIVE

The objective of this lesson is to reflect upon the relationship between love and faith, and how in Christian context one cannot be had without the other.

OPENING PRAYER

> *God, you sent your Son into the world that we might live through him. May we abide in his risen life so that we may bear the fruit of love for one another and know the fullness of joy. Amen.*[109]

READING PHILEMON 4-7

Read verses 4-7 three times in three different versions of the Bible. Pay particular attention to the differences in the way each version translates verse 6. Make notes on the differences.

LESSON

PRAYER AND THANKSGIVING

Paul begins by reminding Philemon, if he doesn't already know, that Paul remembers Philemon in his prayers. It is clear from Paul's letters that prayer is critically significant for him and that it was a daily spiritual discipline for him. It is not too difficult

---

109 *The Revised Commentary Lectionary*, http://lectionary.library.van-derbilt.edu/prayers.php?id=90.

to imagine that Paul spent much time in prayer each day. This would have been especially true in prison, where there would have been little else to do. Prayer sustained Paul and his mission—it was bathed and guided in the Apostle's prayers as well as many others who prayed for Paul.

Paul tells Philemon that in his prayers he thanks God for him. It was noted in the commentary on Colossians 1:3-8 (pp. 16 & 17) that Paul never directly thanks anyone for their work and faithfulness; he always thanks God for their human endeavors on behalf of the gospel. What God is doing through others on behalf of Jesus Christ in this world is God's doing. God deserves the thanks. It is such thanksgiving, directed toward God, that makes our kingdom work rewarding. What a privilege and joy it is to know that others thank God for our faithfulness. It may be that Paul had in mind the words of Jesus in the Sermon on the Mount, "Let your light shine before others, so that they may see your good works and give glory to your Father in heaven" (Matthew 5:16).

The followers of Jesus are not faithful for the kudos. God gets the glory, and God will reward us at the appropriate time.

FAITH IS REVEALED IN LOVE

Paul thanks God for Philemon's love and faith. Love is mentioned first because it is the outworking of faith. Philemon's faith in Christ is demonstrated to be genuine because of his love for his fellow believers. Paul is not specific about how Philemon demonstrated his love toward the believers, but his way of life in the church community left no doubt as to the depth of his faith. Here Paul reflects the words of 1 John 4:18, "Little children, let us love, not in word or speech, but in truth and action." Paul's introductory comments in his letter are not perfunctory. The themes mentioned at the beginning of his letters are always connected to what he writes in the body of the letter. Seven terms are worth noting: "love," "prayers," "sharing," "partnership," "good," "goodness," "heart," "refreshed," and "brother."[110] Paul will use these themes to make his appeal to Philemon.

If love is the outworking of faith, then faith is necessary to love as Christ loved as a follower of Jesus. Jesus himself stressed that the kind of love he calls his followers to demonstrate must be rooted in the active life of faith. Non-believers can certainly love, but Christian love can only be exercised in the context of discipleship. In the Sermon on the Mount, Jesus states, "For if you love those who love you, what reward do you have? Do not even the tax collectors do the same? And if you greet only your brothers and sisters, what more are you doing than others? Do not even the Gentiles do the same?" (Matthew 5:46-47). The kind of faithful love Jesus commands is the kind of love that sent him to the cross. Thus Christian faith and Christian love need each other. One cannot exist without the other.

Philemon has publicly demonstrated his faith and his love as a follower of Jesus. As Onesimus is now a member of the Body of Christ, Paul will appeal to Philemon to demonstrate publicly that same faith and love toward his returning slave. When Paul refers to Philemon's "sharing of your faith," he does not have in mind Philemon's public witness outside the church, but within the community of faith. The word translated "sharing" by the NRSV is *koinonia*, often translated in the New Testament as "fellowship." It is in that sharing of Christ's life together that the church witnesses to the reconciliation God desires to bring to the world in Jesus Christ. What happens in the church makes a difference for its witness in the world. Faith in Christ means faithfulness in the Body of Christ and the sharing of a mutual love whose witness calls all those outside the Body to believe and join the fellowship characterized by sacrificial love.

---

110 Ralph P. Martin, *Colossians and Philemon* (Grand Rapids: Eerdmans, 1973), p. 159.

DISCUSSION QUESTIONS

1. In today's church we often separate the words "faith" and "faithfulness." For many, faith is what one believes and faithfulness is what one does. But the Bible makes no distinction. Dietrich Bonhoeffer said it best, "Only he who believes obeys and only he who obeys believes."[111] Why do you think Christians often separate the two?

2. The church is not a perfect place to be sure, but it is a place where love is to be seen in action. What are some of the ways we fail to love one another in the Body of Christ?

3. In Philemon, Paul is going to urge Philemon to be reconciled to Onesimus because that is the essence of Christ's work— "God was in Christ reconciling the world to himself" (2 Corinthians 5:19). What kinds of things keep estranged Christians from working out their serious disagreements?

EXERCISE

Is there a fellow Christian in your life from whom you have been estranged? Think about how you might make amends. It's irrelevant who is at fault. What can you do to begin a conversation that might lead to reconciliation? A phone call? An email? An invitation to meet for coffee? Reconciliation is hard work, but Jesus went to the cross to reconcile the world to God. How might you participate in the ministry of reconciliation on a personal level?

HISTORICAL/THEOLOGICAL REFLECTION

My friend and blogger, Ted Gossard writes the following:

> *"Blessed are the merciful, for they will be shown mercy"* (Matthew 5:7).
> The new life in Christ has one sure sign of existing: love for God and love for God's children (1 John 5). And this love is evidenced in our obedience to God's commandments. Love and truth are always together in scripture. We also must re-

---

111 *The Cost of Discipleship.*

member that final, thorough, infallible judgment belongs to God alone. And that in fact we're called to embrace the mercy which triumphs over judgment in extending that mercy to those we instead could judge (James 2).

If we've experienced God's mercy and grace, then we should be extending that to others in little as well as big ways. We must be friendly. There is no such thing as truth apart from the love which accompanies it. Truth is nothing more than falsehood apart from that love. In fact such "truth" is a lie, an illusion and I'm afraid often a facade for the real agenda.

Truth exists first in the Trinity of God: The Father, the Son, and the Holy Spirit. And that is a communion of Love. Grace and mercy extended to us in and through Jesus to enter into that very Communion.

On the flip side, love strictly speaking does not exist at all apart from truth, ultimately the truth that is in Jesus. Not to say there isn't genuine love in existence through creation. But the love from which that comes from will bring us face to face with truth. The farther apart love is from truth, the less genuine that love is.

In all of this we need God's mercy and grace. Each of us need that just as much as the next person. A mercy and grace we're to extend to others, always, no matter what– in the truth that is in Jesus.[112]

Ted reminds us that our faith, what we believe to be true, must be worked out in faithfulness to one another in the Body of Christ. His words harken us once again of the words of Jesus in the Gospel of John 13:35, "By this everyone will know that you are my disciples, if you have love for one another."

Closing Prayer

> *Lord, because you have made me, I owe you the whole of my love; because you have redeemed me, I owe you the whole*

---

112 "The Love We Need, and Are to Offer to Others," https://communityofjesus.wordpress.com/2015/07/29/the-love-we-need-and-are-to-offer-to-others/.

of myself; because you have promised so much, I owe you my whole being. Moreover, I owe you as much more love than myself as you are greater than I, for whom you gave yourself and to whom you promised yourself. I pray you, Lord, make me taste by love what I taste by knowledge; let me know by love what I know by understanding. I owe you more than my whole self, but I have no more, and by myself I cannot render the whole of it to you. Draw me to you, Lord, in the fullness of your love. I am wholly yours by creation; make me all yours, too, in love. Amen.[113]

---

113 Anselm of Canterbury (1033-1109), http://www.faithandworship. com/early_Christian_prayers.htm.

OBJECTIVE

In this lesson participants will be challenged to reflect upon what it means for Christians to truly belong to the family of God, and the implications of being brothers and sisters in Christ through faith in Jesus.

OPENING PRAYER

> *O God, make the door of this house wide enough to receive all who need human love and fellowship; narrow enough to shut out all envy, pride, and strife. Make its threshold smooth enough to be no stumbling-block to children, nor to straying feet, but rugged and strong enough to turn back the tempter's power. God make the door of this house the gateway to your eternal kingdom.* [114]

READING PHILEMON 8-22

Read these verses several times in three different translations. Take special note of the family terminology that Paul employs in this section of his letter. Reflect on why Paul uses such familiar language in the letter.

---

114 Thomas, Ken (16-37-1711), *The Complete Book of Christian Prayer* (New York: Continuum, 1995), p. 431.

LESSON

A HEARTFELT APPEAL

Marianne Meye Thompson points out that there were three approaches to persuasive argument (rhetoric) in Paul's day: the *pathos* (Greek for "suffering") approach which attempts to engender sympathy in those listening, the *ethos* (Greek for "custom" or "character") approach in which the speaker presents themselves in a way that inspires confidence in the hearers, and the *logos* (in Greek "word" or "reason") approach, which offers logical argumentation as a way to convince the audience of the reasonable nature of the position being commended. Thompson is certainly correct to say that Paul take the *pathos* approach in his attempt to persuade Philemon in the letter.[115] Paul uses the language of family, something quite common in the early church to appeal to Philemon on behalf of Onesimus. Paul refers to himself as Onesimus' father and refers to Onesimus as "my child," and he addresses Philemon as brother in verse 20. Thus, in no uncertain terms Paul is making the concerns over Onesimus a family matter because Onesimus is now part of the church family. He is not to be viewed as an outsider, but as one who is related to Paul and Philemon and to the church in his house by virtue of their common faith in Jesus Christ. Three things should be noted here.

First, in other letters Paul refers to himself as the father of his converts and his converts as his children— "I am not writing this to you ashamed, but to admonish you as my beloved children. for though you might have ten thousand guardians in Christ, you do not have many fathers. Indeed, in Christ Jesus I became your father through the gospel." (1 Corinthians 4:14-15, (see also 2 Corinthians 6:13, Galatians 4:19; Philippians 2:22). There can be little doubt that Paul had a sense of paternal responsibility over those who came to faith in Jesus through his evangelistic work. As

---

115 Marianne Meye Thompson, *Colossians and Philemon* (Grand Rapids: Eerdmans, 2005), p. 217.

it is simply not enough for a good father to assist in conceiving a child so that they may be born, it is important for fathers to nurture their children toward maturity. In the same way, Paul was not only interested in bringing people into the new birth in Jesus Christ, but he wanted to make sure he and others nurtured them in the faith that they might grow into Christ and be faithful and mature disciples. In mind here perhaps is Psalm 1 where it is said that those who delight in the Lord are "like trees planted by streams of water, which yield their fruit in its season, and their leaves do not whither" (Psalm 1:3).

Second, it was quite out of custom in the Roman world to refer to a slave as a child. Throughout the ancient literature of Greece and Rome slaves are viewed very negatively. In fact a slave had no identity of his or her own, but was imposed upon the slave in that the owner named him or her.[116] Slaves may have been members of the household, but legally that did not make them part of the family. Legally they were property to be treated as the head of the household wished.

Yet, Paul is now speaking of Onesimus as part of his Christian family and trying to persuade Onesimus to do the same. Indeed, he hopes that Philemon welcomes Onesimus back to his home as a brother in Christ. Once again, this does not necessarily suggest that Paul is trying to convince Philemon to free Onesimus. While that cannot be ruled out Paul's language is not specific enough to be certain.

Perhaps Paul is also using family language in referring to himself as an "old man" in verse 9. Some may take this as somewhat manipulative on Paul's part, but in Paul's world elders commanded a great deal of respect. Paul is then reminding Philemon of the importance of advice as one who has experienced many years of life and ministry in the name of Jesus.

Third, Paul makes it very clear to Philemon that how he deals with Onesimus is his decision— "though I am bold enough to

---

116 Thomas Weidemann, *Greek and Roman Slavery* (Baltimore: Johns Hopkins University Press, 1981), p. 1.

command you to do your duty, yet I would rather appeal to you on the basis of love, (verse 8), and then, "I preferred to do nothing without your consent, in order that your good deed might be voluntary and not something forced" (verse 14).

Paul is appealing to his apostolic authority in suggesting he could command Philemon to fulfill his wishes concerning Onesimus, but that would be out of character with his *pathos* approach of engendering sympathy in Philemon. Compulsion does not produce sympathy. In fact, it often makes one even more callous. Moreover, such compulsion would undoubtedly put Philemon in a difficult position once he returned to the household. Paul knows that the only way to resolve the situation is through genuine reconciliation. Onesimus can only flourish in Philemon's household as a welcomed and accepted member of the family.

WHAT'S IN A NAME?

It is important to remember that it was the head of the household who usually named his slaves. A slave sold from one house to another could expect to receive a new and different name in each household. Paul uses the meaning of Onesimus' name as another way to appeal to Philemon of the changed status of Onesimus as a follower of Jesus and as a member of the church family.[117]

Onesimus' name means profitable. Now that Philemon's slave as become a Christian, Paul indicates how useful (if something is useful it is profitable) Onesimus is now that he is a believer. Whatever the nature of Onesimus' previous behavior that led him to run away from Philemon or simply leave the house in seeking Paul's help as one who might intercede, Onesimus' behavior made him useless to Philemon as Paul indicates in verse eleven. But now he is useful both to Paul and Philemon, and Philemon needs to consider that Onesimus' change of status as a Christian will make for a change in his service to Philemon and to the gospel. Thompson states,

---

117 Ben Witherington III, *The Letters to Philemon, the Colossians, and the Ephesians* (Grand Rapids: Eerdmans, 2007), p. 74.

It is as a Christian, a brother in the Lord, Paul's own child, that Onesimus has taken on his particular usefulness to Paul. Paul's argument reflects the traditional idea, expounded in Aristotle, that "property is a collection of...tools, and a slave is an inanimate piece of property." But Paul's is not a utilitarian interest in Onesimus: he has acquired not a new tool but a new son in the Lord.[118]

For Paul the name "Christian" is a game-changer in the relationship between Philemon and his slave. Onesimus may have remained Philemon's slave. We do not know. But it is his new status as a follower of Jesus that first, foremost, and centrally determine the relationship and status between fellow believers. Given names whether from a master or a father and one's status whether slave or free are ordered and reordered in the context of the name Christian. Since Onesimus is now Philemon's brother, he must first relate to him as a Christian brother and not a slave. Had Philemon at this point been familiar with Paul's letter to Colossians, he would have known what that meant, for Christians are to "bear with one another and, if anyone has a complaint against another, forgive each other; just as the Lord has forgiven you, so you also must forgive" (Colossians 3:13).

Philemon must now see Onesimus through the eyes of Christ.

SACRIFICIAL RECONCILIATION

In his appeal to Philemon, Paul continues to appeal to Philemon's sympathies. As has been said we do not know the nature of Onesimus' offense, but whatever it was and whatever it cost, Paul writes to Philemon and says, "If he has wronged you in any way, or owes you anything, charge that to my account" (verse 17). Here Paul is demonstrating the way of Jesus. In the parable of the Good Samaritan the Samaritan not only stops to help the beaten man by the side of the road but takes him to an inn and promises to reimburse the innkeeper for expenses used to care for him (Luke

---

118 Marianne Meye Thompson, *Colossians and Philemon* (Grand Rapids: Eerdmans, 2005), p. 291.

10-25-37). It is most clearly and centrally seen in Jesus' own sacrifice that paid the debt for humanity on the cross. In this Colossians once again comes to mind— "And when you were dead in trespasses and the uncircumcision of your flesh, God made you alive together with him, when he forgave us all our trespasses, erasing the record that stood against us with its legal demands. He set this aside, nailing it to a cross (Colossians 2:13-14).

Paul and Philemon and now Onesimus have received the amazing grace of God in Christ as Jesus paid the IOU of their sins on the cross. Paul was now prepared to act in keeping with the Lord by offering to take care of Onesimus' IOU to Philemon. Would Philemon now make good on his IOU to Paul, which Paul reminds him of in verse 19, by granting Paul's request to Philemon concerning Onesimus? Paul has offered sacrificial reconciliation to Philemon. Would Philemon do the same for Onesimus?

Paul is putting himself in Onesimus' place, offering to pay for the injury (monetary and other) done to Philemon by his slave. Jesus did even more for Paul; Paul could do no less for Onesimus. In a rephrasing of 2 Corinthians 5:19— "God is in Christ reconciling the world to himself"—N. T. Wright comments on Philemon 18, "God is in Paul reconciling Philemon to Onesimus."[119]

The work of reconciliation continues.

DISCUSSION QUESTIONS

1. In what ways would you describe the church as a family? What would be different about the contemporary church if its members truly viewed themselves as family members?

2. Whether we want to admit it or not there are plenty of Onesimuses in our churches today. Fellow Christians who are ignored by the cliques of the church, people who for whatever reasons seem to exist on the margins of the community and are not embraced by other members. Who are the Onesimuses in

---

119 N.T. Wright, *Colossians and Philemon,* Tyndale New Testament Commentaries (Downers Give: IVP Academic, 2008), p. 187.

our churches today? What should we do in welcoming them as equal members of the Body of Christ?

3. Sacrificial reconciliation is difficult work, but our Christian faith is founded upon it. Paul models the example of Jesus in offering to take Onesimus' place to pay any debts he may owe to Philemon. Where have you seen this kind of sacrificially reconciling work in the church today? Why is it not seen more often?

EXERCISE

Think of a way that you can exercise sacrificial reconciliation in your church. It can be monetary but doesn't have to be. There are plenty of ways to show the way of Jesus to others. Ask yourself, how can I give in a way that is truly sacrificial? What am I willing to give up in order to practice sacrificial reconciliation in my life?

HISTORICAL/THEOLOGICAL REFLECTION

Many years ago when I was a college student, I knew a Christian man who practiced extravagant generosity in his life. One day, I saw him on campus with his brand new Ford Fairmont (Fairmont! Now that was a long time ago!) I paused in my daily trek to the library to admire his new and shiny blue vehicle.

This man had a neighbor; an elderly widow, who drove a car that had seen its better days, in fact even its worst days were behind it. He was quite the amateur mechanic, and every time her car had a problem, he would fix it for her free of charge. He always tried to keep her from reimbursing him for the parts, since her income was quite fixed and meager, but she insisted; it was her way of giving back to him in gratitude for his generosity.

One day, on a Saturday, as he was one again in his garage working on her vehicle, he realized that he was able to deal with her car and its problems and its stalling by the side of the road much better than she. He went into the house, retrieved his car keys, and drove his brand new Ford Fairmount over to her house and offered (and insisted) to trade her car for his. In that moment, this man embodied the kind of extravagant generosity that should and must characterize all followers of Jesus Christ.[120]

CLOSING PRAYER

> *Jesus, tender and loving Lamb of God, Utmost Sacrifice of all sacrifices, your glory is reverberated in the highest. Being preoccupied with my well-being, you chose to self-sacrifice Yourself, Setting aside all Your personal glories. I thank You Lord Jesus for Your act of love! Your action has drawn me closer to You. Teach me to model in smaller things, to sacrifice in order to help others, guiding my soul to endure abstinence. Lamb of God, I thank you endlessly!*[121]

---

120 Allan R. Bevere, "Extravagant Generosity" in Robert Schnase, *Five Practices: Manual and Media*. Nashville: Abingdon, 2008, p. 73.
121 Catholic Online, http://www.catholic.org/prayers/prayer. php?p=1617.

LESSON 4
FINAL GREETINGS AND BENEDICTION
(PHILEMON 23-25)

OBJECTIVE

In this lesson, readers will reflect upon the importance of re-membering that the gospel of Jesus Christ is personal in character and that no one individual can do the work of the gospel alone. While God in Jesus Christ is at the center of the gospel, it must not be forgotten that God has sent Jesus because all of creation, and most importantly human beings, are at the center of God's atten-tion. As the New Testament reminds us, we love God because God first loved us (1 John 4:10). The gospel is personal; and the work of offering the personal nature of the gospel cannot be accomplished in isolation. Even the great Apostle Paul needed help.

OPENING PRAYER

> *Almighty God, you teach us in your word that love is the fulfilling of the law: grant that we may love you with all our heart and our neighbors as ourselves; through Jesus Christ our Lord, who is alive with you in the unity of the Holy Spirit, one God now and forever. Amen.*[122]

READING PHILEMON 23-25

As you read Paul's final greetings at the end of the letter, take note of the names mentioned. Have you read these names before in the New Testament? If you think so, where? Why do you think it was important for Paul to mention these individuals specifically?

---

122 *Liturgy,* http://liturgy.co.nz/reflection/634.html.

LESSON

GREETINGS FROM PAUL'S FELLOW LABORERS

As we discovered in Colossians, it was customary for the writer of a letter to send greetings from persons known to the writer and possibly to the recipients. Paul sends such greetings at the close of his letter to Philemon.

Epaphras is named first. Paul refers to him as "my fellow prisoner" (verse 23). This has caused confusion as to the status of both Epaphras and Aristarchus. In Colossians, nothing is mentioned of Epaphras' imprisonment, though Aristarchus is referred to as such. Here in Philemon it is completely the opposite—Epaphras is the prisoner, but not Aristarchus. Some have suggested that the reference to prisoner should not be taken literally. Rather, Paul is referring to Epaphras as a fellow prisoner to the powers of the present evil age.[123] It is impossible to know what is exactly going on here, but it certainly can be said that Paul's companions in mission were also at risk of imprisonment and possible flogging, and yes, they were locked in battle with the principalities and powers of this world who feverishly attempt to undo God's plans in Jesus Christ. The other names mentioned in Paul's final greetings are also mention at the end of Colossians (4:7-17). Who they were may be reviewed in the commentary on Colossians above.

After Jesus, Paul gets all the attention in the New Testament, and that is understandable. But it must never be forgotten that Paul did not act alone. He may have been the central figure during his missionary journeys and travels, but without his companions along the way, it is doubtful that Paul would have had the success that he did. It's all too easy to pass over the names Paul mentions in the final greetings of his letters, but we dare not do so. We must pause, read their names out loud and thank God for those faithful missionaries who labored and suffered with the great Apostle. And

---

123 N.T. Wright, *Colossians and Philemon,* Tyndale New Testament Commentaries (Downers Give: IVP Academic, 2008), p. 191.

perhaps that is the best way to end the lesson, coming around full circle from a plea to treat a slave as a brother and also a reminder that those who work in the shadows of ministry are just as necessary as those who get all the attention. It is in Philemon that we get a small glimpse into one attempt by Paul to work out in the life of the church the affirmation of Colossians 3:11—"there is no longer Greek and Jew, circumcision, and uncircumcision, barbarian, Scythian, slave and free; but Christ is all and in all!"

DISCUSSION QUESTIONS

1. Name the fellow laborers you know who do their work faithfully and often behind the scenes who seldom get kudos for their work, and are often content to be anonymous. What kinds of work for the church have they accomplished?
2. How can we recognize the Aristarchuses and Demases of the church who are not at the center of attention? How can we give them the thanks they deserve without putting them publicly on the spot embarrassing them?

EXERCISE

Send a thank you note this week to one person in the church who labors faithfully and quietly for the church. Tell them how important their work is for Christ and his Body in the world.

HISTORICAL/THEOLOGICAL REFLECTION

John Wesley was onboard a ship bound for the Georgia colony in early 1736 when a ferocious storm shredded the main sail and flooded the decks.

Many of the English passengers aboard screamed in terror that they would soon be swallowed by the deep. But a group of Moravian missionaries from Germany calmly sang throughout the squall. They were unafraid of death, an astound John Wesley later recounted in his journal.

That journey marked Wesley's first significant encounter with a small Protestant movement that would have an enormous influence on his ministry and the Methodist movement he started.

Two years later, a disheartened Wesley was back in England wrestling with his Christian faith after a miserable time in Georgia. On May 24, 1738, friends prevailed upon him to attend a Moravian society meeting on Aldersgate Street in London.

Many United Methodists can recite what happened next. That night, upon hearing Martin Luther's preface to Romans, Wesley wrote, "I felt my heart strangely warmed. I felt I did trust in Christ alone for salvation." Wesley's spiritual awakening was a turning point in his life, and arguably it might not have happened without the Moravians.[124]

Closing Prayer

God of unsearchable mystery and light, your weakness is greater than our strength, your foolishness brings all our cleverness to naught, your gentleness confounds the power we would claim. You call first to be last and last to be first, servant to be leader and ruler to be underling of all. Pour into our hearts the wisdom of your Word and Spirit, that we may know your purpose and live to your glory. Amen.[125]

---

124 umg.org, http://www.umc.org/news-and-media/a-little-known-big-influence-on-john-wesley.

125 *The Revised Common Lectionary*, http://lectionary.library.vanderbilt.edu/prayers.php?id=220.

Appendix A:

Participatory Study Method

How can I get more from my Bible reading?

There is no shortcut in Bible study. If you want to find what God has for you in Scripture you will have to dig. There are some things you can do to make your study time more profitable. In this appendix you will find an outline to an approach to Bible study that can help you both with devotional reading and with deeper study.

PREPARATION

Gather Materials – have pen, paper, highlighters or other markers and all materials you will need for study available.

Conditions – Find a place where you can study. If you study well with music playing, put some on. If you prefer quiet, arrange for a quiet place.

Resources – Get a small, well-selected set of study materials. For suggestions see the resource list in appendix B.

Prayer – As you begin your study, consider the premise that Scripture comes to us as God-breathed, and therefore it is "useful for teaching for reproof, for correction, and for training in righteousness, so that everyone who belongs to God may be proficient, equipped for every good work" (2 Timothy 3:16- 17 NRSV). Keeping in mind this word, share in this prayer:

Eternal God, in the reading of the Scripture, may your word be heard; in the meditations of our hearts, may your word be known; and in the faithfulness of our lives, may your word be shown. Amen.

(Chalice Worship, 384).

GET AN OVERVIEW OF THE PASSAGE

Read the passage multiple times. Any number from three times up will help. Memorizing is useful, at least of key texts. (This will also require you to select key texts.) Read from different Bible versions, to help you with your concentration, and to open up different ways of understanding the passage. At this point don't use commentaries, study notes, your concordance, or anything which takes your concentration off of the passage you are studying.

STUDY THE BACKGROUND

Find out who wrote the passage, to whom it was written, what is the situation being addressed, and what type of literature it is.

MEDITATE, QUESTION, RESEARCH, COMPARE (REPEAT AS NEEDED)

Meditate on the passage. If you are having difficulty meditating, think about telling someone else about the passage, such as a friend in need of encouragement, someone who is struggling with their faith or asking questions about faith, or a child. Think: What questions might they ask about this passage? You can formulate thought questions or fact questions. Fact questions focus on what the author is actually saying. Thought questions may lead you to other revelations that lay well beyond the intended statement of the passage.

You might consider creating an outline of the passage, compare it with other Scriptures or with the writings of figures in church history, or even to current experience.

Ask: What similar experience are we having today? Could this help me better understand the passage. For example, if you have had a vision, might this help you understand the vision recorded in Ezekiel 1? Ask your friends about experiences they have had. You might consult historical figures such as: Jerome, Aquinas,

Teresa of Avila, Augustine, Martin Luther, John Wesley, John Calvin, Karl Barth, and many others.

SHARE YOUR THOUGHTS

Ask yourself how this text has been applied in your experience. Get to know the person you are sharing with. Share your experience and then the text. Always work from your own personal experience with God. Store up the experiences your friends share with you to use in studying further Scripture.

The purpose of sharing is not just to help others with your own insight. It is also intended to provide a check on what you think you have learned. It is easy to get off track in independent Bible study. Sharing helps keep you a part of the community. Make sure that some of your sharing is with people who have experience and training in study. Training and degrees do not guarantee accuracy, but it does provide a valuable check.

EXAMPLE PASSAGE 1 KINGS 19:11-18

1. Begin your study with prayer.
2. Read the passage several times. Can you tell this story in your own words?
   a) Read 1 Kings 17-19. Check a Bible dictionary or study Bible for the background of 1Kings.
   b) Consider how Elijah feels through this experience.
   c) Consider what God is trying to accomplish by giving Elijah these experiences.
   d) How did Elijah know the Lord was not in the wind, the earthquake or the fire?
   e) Can the Lord appear in such violent events? (Use your concordance, looking up wind, fire, and earthquake.)
   f) Does God respond to Elijah's complaint? (Only indirectly; he gives him a task.)
   g) Is Elijah as much alone as he feels he is? (No, there are 7,000 more faithful people, v. 18.)

h)   What other Bible characters have experienced something similar to this? (Daniel 3—the fiery furnace.)

i)   What people in church history may have experienced something similar to this? (Any martyr or person who has suffered persecution.)

j)   Have you experienced similar feelings? Have you ever felt completely alone in your faith?

3.   Share your experiences!!

EXAMPLE PRAYER FOR BIBLE STUDY

Lord, take from me any thought habits which will keep me from hearing. Make me open to your voice and your voice alone. Lord, help me to accept your people as my brothers and sisters in your kingdom and let me learn and grow from both their weaknesses and their strengths. Lord, I trust you to reveal yourself to your people the way you know is best. Let your will be done. Lord, let me not only recognize but obey your voice. Let my actions be conformed to your will. Help me to love my neighbor as myself. In Jesus' name, Amen.

Appendix B:

Tools for Bible Study

The following are some suggested resources for Bible study. They fall into eight categories:

BIBLE VERSIONS

You will need a Bible version that you can understand without having to consult an English dictionary too often.

✓ For quick reading (overview):

» *Contemporary English Version* (CEV)

3rd or 4th grade reading level; high degree of accuracy within the context of its aim for easy readability.

» *The Cotton Patch Version* by Clarence Jordan

An interpretive paraphrase reflecting rural Georgian dialect and culture.

» *The Message*

Heavily paraphrased with cultural terms translated. This version is fun to read, but will tend to obscure elements of the original cultures.

» *New Living Translation* (NLT)

A more accurate revision of the Living Bible. This is the easy-reading Bible for evangelical Christians.

» *Today's New International Version*

Shows its relationship to the popular NIV in many wordings, but uses simplified language and sentence structure in many cases.

✓ For study or reading:

» *Common English Bible* (CEB)

A new translation sponsored by Mainline Protestant publishing houses, the CEB attempts to combine high level scholarship with readability. The New Testament was published in 2010, with the complete Bible available in 2011.

» *New International Version* (NIV)

The NIV is a dynamic equivalent translation of the Bible that is popular among evangelical Christians. A new revision of this translation appeared in electronic form in 2010 and will be available in print in 2011

» *New Revised Standard Version* (NRSV)

The descendant of the Revised Standard Version, it is the Bible of choice for mainline Christians needing a study Bible. It is known for its attempt to use gender neutral language where appropriate.

» *Revised English Bible* (REB)

This version was translated by an interdenominational committee with interfaith review, that exhibits the different texture of British English.

» *New American Standard Bible* (NASB)

A very formal rendering of the original languages, the NASB has its roots in conservative evangelicalism. It can be wooden and difficult to read.

STUDY BIBLES

Study Bibles usually contain introductory articles giving Bible backgrounds, information on methodology and overviews of various themes in the Bible. They will also include introductions to each book and comments on difficult passages. Study Bibles will reflect religious views of editors and authors, some more than others. Care should be taken to distinguish the Biblical text from the comments, and facts and opinions within the comments.

✓ *New Interpreter} Study Bible* (NRSV)

This new study Bible includes extensive historical and theological annotations, good introductions and outlines, and excursuses giving further background and insight regarding particular themes and passages.

✓ *New Oxford Annotated Bible* (NRSV)

A standard scholarly study Bible, often used in universities and seminaries.

✓ *HarperCollins Study Bible* (NRSV)

Carrying the sponsorship of the Society of Biblical Literature, it has Mainstream or liberal notes with acknowledgment of more conservative options.

✓ *Oxford Study Bible* (REB)

✓ *The NIV Study Bible* (Zondervan)

Popular among evangelicals, bringing a more conservative approach to the Bible.

✓ *ESV Study Bible*

A new Reformed standard study.

✓ *NLT Study Bible*

Based on the popular, easy-to-read New Living Translation, this evangelical study Bible provides extensive notes on both background and application.

BIBLE HANDBOOKS

Bible handbooks provide historical and cultural information, usually with a number of general articles and then comments on particular books and passages. Using a Bible handbook along with your Bible is like having a Bible with study notes, though usually having a handbook in a separate volume will mean that the handbook contains more exhaustive information. Bible handbooks, like study Bibles, will reflect religious presuppositions of the editors. Use them carefully.

✓ Mainstream and/or Liberal

»   *The Cambridge Companion to the Bible O:iford Companion to the Bible*
✓ Moderate
    »   *Eerdman's Handbook to the Bible*
✓ Conservative
    »   *Zondervan's Handbook to the Bible*

BACKGROUND DOCUMENTS

✓   Pritchard, James. *Ancient Near Eastern Texts*

Large, expensive, hard cover but a tremendous resource for the Bible student.

✓   Pritchard, James. *The Ancient Near East, Volume 1, An Anthology of Texts and Pictures*

(Both 1958 and 1975 editions still available)

✓   Charlesworth, James H. *The Old Testament Pseudepigrapha* (2 volumes).

This work is a standard for editions of these extra-biblical works.

BIBLE COMMENTARIES

Bible commentaries are designed to provide introductions, background, and interpretation of biblical texts. They come in many forms, ranging from one-volume efforts to commentaries on individual books. Many commentaries appear in sets, but with few exceptions, when purchasing commentaries on individual books of the Bible it is better to buy these individually rather than in sets. There are a few exceptions, such as with the New Interpreter's Bible, which is something of a hybrid. It is important to stay away from older, dated commentaries, except perhaps for devotional or theological reasons. In many online programs you will find commentaries such as Matthew Henry's, which is in public domain and thus free to publish without copyright infringement. It is, however, an 18th century product. A good place to start for any library is a solid, up-to-date one-volume commentary.

✓ Mainstream

» *New Interpreter's Bible*, 12 volumes (Abingdon)

A replacement for the venerable Interpreter's Bible, this is a mainstream commentary set drawing its authors from across the Christian community, including evangelical, mainline, Catholic, and Orthodox scholars.

» *New Interpeter's One Volume Commentary* (Abingdon)

Based on the principles of the much larger multi-volume edition, it is a completely new commentary and not simply an abridgement.

» *HarperCollins Bible Commentary* (HarperOne)

As with the HarperCollins Bible Dictionary, this commentary is sponsored by the Society of Biblical Literature.

» *People's New Testament Commentary of the New Testament* (WJK Press)

This commentary on the New Testament is written by two Disciples of Christ scholars, Fred Craddock and Eugene Boring.

» *The New Jerome Bible Commentary*, 3rd edition (Prentice Hall)

This is a predominantly Roman Catholic commentary, authored and edited by highly regarded critical scholars.

✓ Evangelical

» *Eerdmans Commentary on the Bible*

This work is very compatible with mainstream scholarship, but comes from a publisher that stands as a bridge between evangelical and mainline Protestantism.

» *New Bible Commentary: 21st Century edition* (IVP)

BIBLE CONCORDANCES

Concordances may be exhaustive, complete, or concise. Usage of these terms is not 100% consistent. In addition they may either be either organized by words or topics. Many Bibles contain small, concise concordances. Many study Bibles contain topical concordances. Exhaustive concordances contain every reference to a word listed under every word. Complete concordances contain references to each and every verse, using significant terms, though not necessarily under every word in the verse. Concise concordances contain selective references and may not reference all verses. Topical concordances provide a guide to topics covered by specific texts. This can be helpful, but one must always remember that unlike a typical concordance, which is rooted in word usage, this type is more likely to be driven by theological presuppositions.

Concordances with Greek and/or Hebrew Lexicons can be useful, but one should remember that translation is not as simple as just picking a word from a dictionary definition. Context always determines usage and meaning.

✓ Exhaustive with Greek/Hebrew
    » *Strong's Exhaustive Concordance.*
It is part of the public domain and is regularly reprinted. It is based on the KJV and an older lexicon. It's numbering system and lexicon has served as the model for other concordances
    » *The NIV Exhaustive Concordance* (Zondervan)
Based completely on the NIV, it goes beyond Strong's.
    » *New American Standard Exhaustive Concordance of the Bible/Hebrew-Aramaic and Greek Dictionaries*
    » *New American Standard Strong's Exhaustive Concordance*
Based on the Strong's Concordance system, it is keyed to the NASB.
✓ Exhaustive Concordances
    » *NRSV Concordance Unabridged* (Zondervan)
✓ Complete Concordances
    » *Cruden's Complete Concordance Concordance to the KJV.*
This is an 18th century product, but because it is public domain it is regularly reprinted.
✓ Concise Concordances

»   *The Concise Concordance to the New Revised Standard Version* (Oxford)

✓   Topical Concordances

»   *Holman Concise Topical Concordance* (Holman Reference)

»   *Topical Analysis of the Bible* (Baker)

BIBLE DICTIONARIES

Bible dictionaries provide definitions of various biblical terms, information about places and people, and introductory information about biblical books. Most information contained in a Bible handbook can be found in a Bible dictionary, but it will be organized much differently.

The religious views of authors and editors will impact the content of a Bible dictionary, as it does with a handbook or commentary. When purchasing a Bible dictionary, it is always best to purchase one that has been authored/ edited by reputable scholars, is even-handed in its approach, and is up-to-date.

✓   Mainstream

»   *HarperCollins Bible Dictionary, Revised Edition.* (HarperOne)

»   *A Dictionary of the Bible, 2nd ed.* (Oxford University Press)

Based upon the *Harper-Collins Bible Dictionary,* this is a more up-to-date expansion.

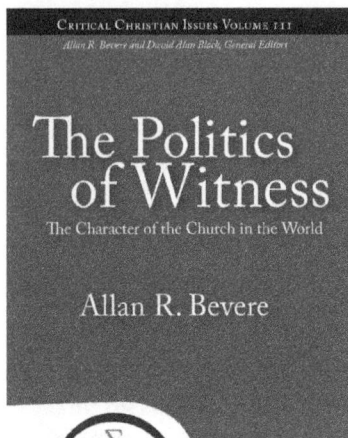

CRITICAL CHRISTIAN ISSUES VOLUME III
Allan R. Bevere and David Alan Black, General Editors

The Politics
of Witness

The Character of the Church in the World

Allan R. Bevere

Σ

AREOPAGUS
CRITICAL CHRISTIAN ISSUES

Allan Bevere, an ecclesial theologian, combines in this book a wonderful "church as politics" with gospel in a wise, warm and challenging manner.

Scot McKnight
Karl A. Olsson Professor
in Religious Studies
North Park Universityy

Bob Cornwall combines the mind of a scholar and the heart of a pastor in this participatory study guide on Ephesians. Demonstrating remarkable skill as a communicator, Bob brings this ancient epistle to our contemporary setting in a way that both illuminates the old letter writer's concerns and enlightens our Christian faith.

Dr. Glen Miles
Senior Minister of Country Club
Christian Church (Disciples of
Christ) of Kansas City

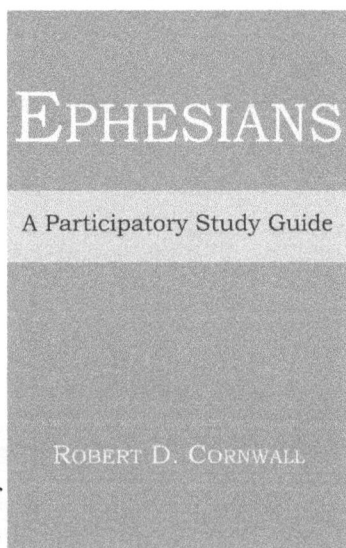

EPHESIANS

A Participatory Study Guide

ROBERT D. CORNWALL

MORE FROM ENERGION PUBLICATIONS

Personal Study

Holy Smoke! Unholy Fire	Bob McKibben	$14.99
The Jesus Paradigm	David Alan Black	$17.99
When People Speak for God	Henry Neufeld	$17.99
The Sacred Journey	Chris Surber	$11.99

Christian Living

It's All Greek to Me	David Alan Black	$3.99
Grief: Finding the Candle of Light	Jody Neufeld	$8.99
My Life Story	Becky Lynn Black	$14.99
Crossing the Street	Robert LaRochelle	$16.99
Life as Pilgrimage	David Moffett-Moore	14.99

Bible Study

From Inspiration to Understanding	Edward W. H. Vick	$24.99
Philippians: A Participatory Study Guide	Bruce Epperly	$12.99
Ephesians: A Participatory Study Guide	Robert D. Cornwall	$12.99
Ecclesiastes: A Participatory Study Guide	Russell Meek	$12.99
The Jesus Manifesto	David Moffett-Moore	$9.99

Theology

Meditations on According to John	Herold Weiss	$14.99
Creation: the Christian Doctrine	Edward W. H. Vick	$12.99
Ultimate Allegiance	Robert D. Cornwall	$9.99
History and Christian Faith	Edward W. H. Vick	$9.99
The Journey to the Undiscovered Country	William Powell Tuck	$9.99
Process Theology	Bruce G. Epperly	$5.99

Ministry

Clergy Table Talk	Kent Ira Groff	$12.99
Wind and Whirlwind	David Moffett-Moore	$9.99

Generous Quantity Discounts Available
Dealer Inquiries Welcome
Energion Publications — P.O. Box 841
Gonzalez, FL 32560
Website: http://energionpubs.com
Phone: (850) 525-3916

www.ingramcontent.com/pod-product-compliance
Lightning Source LLC
LaVergne TN
LVHW011202080426
835508LV00007B/546